You've come up with a brilliant  uct or service you *know* could you currently own a business th dream is to become fabulously lionaire. But how? *How to Mak* has all the answers.

This book is packed with the true stories and proven advice of ordinary people who began with just an idea, a simple product, or a fledgling business and wound up with *millions*. It examines the methods and principles of dozens of successful entrepreneurs, including author Dan Kennedy's surefire, easy-to-follow Millionaire Maker Strategies. It helps you determine which of three paths to success are best for you and guides you step-by-step down that path on your way to fortune. Discover:

- **The 8 best ways to make a fortune from scratch**
- **How to turn a hobby into a million-dollar enterprise**
- **How to sell an existing business for millions**
- **The power of electronic media to help make you rich**
- **The "Million Dollar Rolodex" of contacts and information you can use to get on the road to wealth**

DAN S. KENNEDY is President of Empire Communications Corporation, a mail-order marketing firm, and of LifeTech Broadcasting Corporation, a leading producer of infomercials and video brochures. Kennedy also conducts Millionaire-Maker System Seminars for thousands of people every year.

HOW TO MAKE
MILLIONS
WITH YOUR
IDEAS

AN ENTREPRENEUR'S GUIDE

DAN S. KENNEDY

A PLUME BOOK

PLUME

Published by the Penguin Group
Penguin Books USA Inc., 375 Hudson Street,
New York, New York 10014, U.S.A.
Penguin Books Ltd, 27 Wrights Lane, London W8 5TZ, England
Penguin Books Australia Ltd, Ringwood, Victoria, Australia
Penguin Books Canada Ltd, 10 Alcorn Avenue,
Toronto, Ontario, Canada M4V 3B2
Penguin Books (N.Z.) Ltd, 182–190 Wairau Road,
Auckland 10, New Zealand

Penguin Books Ltd, Registered Offices:
Harmondsworth, Middlesex, England

First published by Plume, an imprint of Dutton Signet,
a division of Penguin Books USA Inc.

First Printing, January, 1996
5 7 9 10 8 6 4

 REGISTERED TRADEMARK—MARCA REGISTRADA

LIBRARY OF CONGRESS CATALOGING-IN-PUBLICATION DATA

Kennedy, Dan S.
How to make millions with your ideas : an entrepreneur's guide /
by Dan S. Kennedy.
p. cm.
ISBN 0-452-27316-1
1. New business enterprises. 2. Creative ability in business.
3. Success in business.   I. Title.
HD62.5.K45 1996
658.4'21—dc20   95-9658   CIP

Printed in the United States of America
Set in Times Roman
Designed by Jesse Cohen

PUBLISHER'S NOTE

Contents

HOW TO MAKE
MILLIONS
WITH YOUR
IDEAS

Introduction

SO YOU'VE GOT A "MILLION-DOLLAR IDEA"—NOW WHAT?

Terrific! This is the place and now is the time to turn your ideas into millions of dollars. In this book you're going to meet more than fifty different people who've started with little more than an idea and made millions, many in very short order. Many of these people are my clients and friends, and I know them well. Others are people I've painstakingly researched for this book.

Some of these people or their products or their businesses are famous; most are not. But each person I'll introduce you to demonstrates a different Millionaire-Maker Strategy. One of these strategies or a combination of them is bound to be right for you, too.

It's important for you to immediately understand what this book is *not*. It is *not* another dry, stuffy textbook about how to start, finance, and grow a business, according to Hoyle. If you want to know how to write a business plan, for example, there are plenty of books on library and bookstore shelves that can teach you how to do that. I can't imagine a good reason to write or to publish another one.

Formulas for Success Don't Work, So You Won't Find a Formula Here!

This is *not* a masterfully outlined and organized, step-by-step, 1-2-3 kind of book. Frankly, I don't think people actually get rich that way. Most of the very methodical people I meet are working for wages as somebody else's bean counter.

Success seems to be a more chaotic (and more exciting) process of grabbing this idea from here, that piece of information from over there, goofing this up, seeing that work, and fitting puzzle pieces together until you have just the right combination for your unique situation. Hopefully, this book shortcuts all that for you, but within its pages, you're still going to be grabbing a piece here and a piece there and piecing them together in the way best suited to your purposes. If there was one formula for success, there'd be only one book about it. Formulas for success don't work any more than diets do—if a diet worked, there'd only be *one* diet!

I Wish the Fellows with the Cute Little Patches on the Elbows of Their Corduroy Sports Jackets Would Stay Off the Business Battlefield—Don't You?

Although this is a book about turning ideas into money, it is *not* a book of *ideas*. I have long despised business books written by fuzzy-headed academics, professors in cushy jobs on campuses, accountants, lawyers, and hotshot consultants from big, fat consulting firms, all spouting theories. I speak a lot, often on programs with many other speakers, and I always warn my audiences about the many speakers who ''run businesses only in their nightmares and sell only in their memories.'' Listen, I live and work every day where you do—in the *real* world, where they eat their young. So, here's a little promise: Every single strategy that I point out to you in this book will be one that I have actual, real-world, hands-on experience with, that I've used personally for my businesses or my clients' businesses, and that has been repetitively validated.

Should This Book Have a $10,000 Price Tag?

Most of the information in this book has grown out of my own experience and my consulting activities, and is from my Millionaire-Maker Seminars. It might interest you that people have traveled literally from just about every nook and cranny of the United States and Canada, as well as from a handful of other countries, and paid no less than $295 to as much as $3,495 per person to attend these seminars.

At our $3,495 per-person Millionaire-Maker Direct Marketing Super Conferences, attendees can come back, at an alumni rate of $1,000—and over 90 percent of all attendees have done that at least once, many several times. I don't tell you that to brag. A long time ago, a mentor advised me: Don't worry about impressing people, just get busy inspiring them. So that's what I'm trying to do. I just want you to understand and appreciate the value of what you now hold in your hands. It's much more than the dinky cover price on the book. It's at least the equivalent of a few seminars—$10,000 or so. It represents millions of dollars of mistakes, tens of millions of dollars of notable successes, hundreds of millions of dollars' worth of goods and services sold in sixty-three different business categories.

I hope you'll consider all that, because I know that what you get out of this book will have a relationship to the value that you place on it.

P.S.: Throughout this book, you will find a total of forty-five numbered Millionaire-Maker Strategies. They do not appear in numerical order in the book, as different people's stories illustrate different strategies. At the end of chapter 12, I've reassembled them for you in a logical order, as you might try to apply them to your own idea, product, service, or business. That order is not one of relative importance but one of relationship; it shows how each strategy naturally leads to another.

1

THE EIGHT BEST WAYS TO (STILL) MAKE A FORTUNE FROM SCRATCH IN AMERICA

There must be tens of thousands of different categories and types of businesses, methods, and means of marketing and distributing products and promoting services. Maybe more. With new ones, or, at least, new hybrids being found or figured out every day. We are a very inventive society, especially when it comes to ways to make money.

However, you do not need to be an innovator or pioneer if you carefully evaluate your chief objectives for bringing a product to market or building a business. Money made by pioneering is no more valuable than money made from reliable, predictable means. A dollar is a dollar. A million is a million.

From all of my own entrepreneurial experience—failures as well as successes—and that of my clients, I've identified the eight highest probability areas of opportunity, where millions can still be made from scratch. These days, I try to concentrate my own efforts and business interests in these areas, and to direct my clients into these areas. Why? The key words: "highest probability." Launching a new idea, product, service, or business is risky and problematic enough without doing it in a low probability of success environment. Climbing a huge, forbidding, dangerous mountain is tough enough; why try doing it during the worst snow, rain, ice, and wind storm of the season? So, this chapter serves two purposes. First, it's an overview of the entire book. Second, it sets up these eight categories of high probability entrepreneurial activity, so that you can do just as I do: Adapt your ideas to fit these categories, to bring as many of these categories together as possible.

In chapter 12, I revisit these eight ways with brief, concise lists of the key how-tos for each, revealed mostly by example throughout this book.

High Probability Area of Opportunity #1: Surprise! It's "Ordinary" Businesses!

As you drive down the street tomorrow, on your way to work, or as you run errands and go shopping on Saturday, you'll encounter doughnut shops, restaurants, dry cleaners, bookstores, video rental stores, gift shops, and dozens of other "ordinary" businesses. We give most of these businesses very little thought. These shopkeepers seem to have, in most cases, just created jobs for themselves. In some years they may make as little as $25,000, in their best years no more than three times that, working longer hours and harder than in a comparable job. Nothing very remarkable about any of that, is there?

Yet, here's what's very interesting. Somewhere in America, in every one of those business categories, you can find someone who has found ways to turn an ordinary business into an extraordinary profit machine. I profile several in chapter 2. And, maybe even more interesting, is that more of America's self-made millionaires own and have accumulated their wealth through these ordinary businesses than through any other means.

That local dry cleaner might surprise you. As you drop off your cleaning, you notice that the owner is always there working. What you don't know is that he owns the piece of land or the shopping center where his shop is located, that he has a corporate pension fund that has sheltered a chunk of his earnings from taxes each year for the past ten, and that the dry cleaning business has a collection of extra-profit centers: It refers customers to a carpet cleaning company and receives commissions; aggressively markets fur, suede, and leather cleaning services; sells its own private label brand of spot removers; and has three in-

dependent contractors operating neighborhood pick-up and delivery dry cleaning routes. All things considered, he's doing
about double the normal, one-store average in the dry cleaning
industry. And that, over ten years, has quietly made the owner
rich.

The exciting truth is that you can take just about *any* ordinary
business, do its core business and serve and satisfy customers
just a little bit better than the norm, add clever, extra profit centers to the core business, and manage the money very intelligently—and that business will make you rich.

High Probability Area of Opportunity #2:
The Best Equity Is Exclusivity

If you're just starting to consider any and all business opportunities, you will be confronted, through advertising, business
opportunity and trade shows,. and other sources, with a myriad
of chances to distribute or market other people's products and
services—distributorships, dealerships, franchises, and so on.
You *can* make money this way. But it's very, very difficult to
get rich this way.

Wealth is most often linked to exclusive ownership or control
of a particular concept, product, or service. In chapter 3, I'll
introduce you to people who have followed this path to riches.
Rather than be a cog in someone else's wheel, they made certain
to own the whole wheel outright.

If someone else has control over your destiny, if someone
else can change the economics of your business, alter your marketing rights, impede your creativity, sell the parent company,
or otherwise unexpectedly interfere in your business, you don't
really have your own business. One of the insider secrets to
making millions is doing everything possible to minimize circumstances beyond your control.

High Probability Area of Opportunity #3:
Serve, Serve, Serve

In 1994 almost all the new jobs created in the United States were in the service category. Why? Because those are the businesses expanding most consistently and rapidly. People at all levels of society are unbelievably pressed for time, so they need "servers" to do for them what they do not have time to do for themselves. In chapter 5, I'll show you how to capitalize on this trend by incorporating service elements in *any* business or product.

I'll tell you one illustrative story here, quickly. A client of mine, International Correspondence Schools, has been in the business of selling in-home career training since 1890. These days, one of their most popular home study courses is "Learn to Use a Personal Computer." The product they sell is this home-study course: the books, manuals, videotapes, audiotapes, and computer software. But the service element they've added is ICS ON-LINE, their "electronic campus." Right through the computer, modem, and telephone line, their students can tap into group discussions and classes, leave and receive messages from helpful instructors twenty-four hours a day, share software, and much more. Learn from this example of putting a service element into a product and you'll possess one of the most topical insider secrets for making millions.

High Probability Area of Opportunity #4:
Go Ye Forth and Multiply

One of the great benefits of turning an ordinary business into an extraordinary profit machine and of owning or controlling exclusive products is the ability to get rich through **duplication** and **multiplication.** This *is* a great, big, hungry country of consumers. When you have a business that works in one place, there are almost always dozens, hundreds, thousands, even tens of thousands of other places where it will work, too. Once there was *one* McDonald's—the brothers' original restaurant. One Subway shop. One drive-through car wash. One athletic-shoe store. One fast-photo-processing shop. One of something. One of everything.

In chapter 6, I'll introduce you to some of the "masters" of duplication. You'll see that even simple ideas, products, and services, if properly "packaged," can make you rich through duplication or multiplication.

High Probability Area of Opportunity #5: Go Direct!

Direct Marketing is one of the fastest-growing categories of business. Bypassing all the traditional complexity and costs of manufacturers' representatives or salesforces; wholesalers, jobbers, and other middlemen; retail stores; and brand-identity, image-building advertising, more and more companies are either going directly to the consumers themselves or moving their products and services through established direct marketers.

How do you go direct? With ads or direct-mail campaigns or TV or radio commercials that bring the end user directly in contact with the manufacturer or publisher, with you, usually via an 800 number or the mail. Products that were never sold this way in past years are finding new success in direct marketing— furniture, security systems, computers, food, even automobiles. Services are now sold this way too, such as long-distance telephone and flower delivery. Today, if you want to send someone flowers, you don't schlepp down to the florist shop, you just pick up the phone and call a toll-free number. If you want fresh Maine lobsters for a big cookout this weekend at your home in Nebraska, you don't go to a supermarket or specialty foods store; you call a toll-free number and have the lobsters delivered right to your door. What's next? Maybe *your* fortune.

In chapters 7 and 8, I take you on an eye-opening, opportunity-filled tour of the booming direct-marketing business.

High Probability Area of Opportunity #6:
Profit from the Information Age

The most traded, most consumed, most sought-after, and most valued commodity of our time is not precious stones, oil, or real estate. It is "specialized information." All around you, in every imaginable form, people are profiting by selling what they know or know how to do. Do you know how to plan a fail-safe wedding? Brew beer in a basement? Make famous recipes at home? Lose weight fast? Make money with a computer? Get air travel discounts? Build birdhouses? The list of types of information being turned into profits would itself fill a book bigger than this one.

A quick example: A friend of mine has figured out a way dentists can give complete dental exams in half the usual time. That is his only piece of information. With that piece of information alone, he has developed his own how-to course for dentists, another for dental assistants and dental hygienists, and two video products, and has created a $100,000 per year home-based, part-time business. And, after going through chapter 9, you'll quickly see how he can turn that simple foundation into a million-dollar empire.

High Probability Area of Opportunity #7:
Fame and Fortune Do Go Together

A friend of mine, Paul Hartunian, has made as much as $400,000 in one day. He has been written about in *Forbes* magazine and countless newspapers, been on *The Phil Donahue Show*, many other talk shows, and built two different businesses, all through publicity. By making himself famous—once as an expert in collecting, investing in, trading, and selling celebrity autographs, and once as an expert in meeting and creating relationships with beautiful women—Paul has made a fortune without spending much money at all on advertising. Paul says, "For

$1,000, you can buy one ad in just one newspaper that will be here today, gone tomorrow, or one ad in one magazine that will be gone in a month. For the same $1,000, I can fax 7,000 news releases to 7,000 different media contacts and make the equivalent of hundreds of those ads happen.''

There does seem to be an inexhaustible demand for famous people. There are more TV talk shows on the air than ever before. Talk radio is booming. Magazines like *People* are huge hits. It seems that people are interested in interesting people. In chapter 10, you'll meet people using this interest to their advantage in fascinating, imitatable ways.

High Probability Area of Opportunity #8: Creative, Clever Combinations

It's hard to find an example of just one of these ways of turning ideas into millions. And that fact, in and of itself, points you to one of the greatest millionaire-maker secrets of all.

Three Additional Ways to Look at Businesses and Business Opportunities

As you look at all the examples in this book, you'll see that they fit one of these three categories: product-driven businesses, market-driven businesses, or media-driven businesses.

In a *product-driven business*, the product itself is so appealing, unique, and promotable that it gets sold through a variety of media and methods, to or through a variety of markets. The Nancy Kwan Pearl Cream product mentioned in this book is such a unique cosmetic product that it has the power to drive an entire business. It is sold through direct-response TV commercials and infomercials, print ads in magazines and tabloids, direct-mail, catalogs, health food stores, and drugstores. It has attracted loyal, responsive customers of all ages—teens to senior citizens—who buy it repeatedly and are also receptive to an entire assortment of "Oriental beauty secret" products, Nancy Kwan fitness videos, and other items. The product built the business.

It is relatively rare to find or invent such a powerful product, but when you do, the world is your oyster.

In a *market-driven business*, a particular niche market dictates the development of a product or products or a service or services. The need in the chiropractic and dental professions for advertising and marketing assistance fueled the development of my own SuccessTrak seminar and publishing business, leading to the development of dozens of products and millions of dollars of revenue. A manufacturer I consulted with developed, produced, and sold truck tarping systems exclusively for municipalities' gravel, sand, and refuse trucks, and that market's need was driven by governmental mandates. These are businesses created to serve very specific markets. This is a relatively common although little-noticed, little-understood type of business. And businesses in this category have very high probabilities of success.

In a *media-driven business*, a variety of products and services, even apparently unrelated products, or multiple businesses, are all sold through one primary medium. The Guthy-Renker Corporation mentioned in this book sells Victoria Principal cosmetics and has built a cosmetics business with a product line of over 100 products exclusively through infomercials and home shopping channels. But they also sell a motor oil additive, exercise and fitness videos, self-improvement courses, and golf products, and have a number of businesses within their business. The only commonality is the media that drives all the sales. Media-driven businesses are modern, high-tech distribution businesses. The entrepreneur is not a specialist in any particular product or service; instead, he is a specialist in a particular method of distribution. To me, these are the most interesting and exciting businesses. And businesses in this category are often the ones that go from zero to millions at the fastest pace.

By understanding these categories, and the high probability types, you will look at all businesses differently and mold your own new or existent, reinvented enterprise to fit a desirable category and a high probability type.

2

HOW YOU CAN TURN AN "ORDINARY" BUSINESS INTO AN EXTRAORDINARY MONEYMAKING MACHINE

As I said in the first chapter, one of the most accessible, practical ways to make a fortune is with an "ordinary" business. It's very difficult (although not impossible) to create an as-yet-unseen, revolutionary product or service. But you can take what you already have, even though there may be lots of competition, and transform it into a revolutionary leader.

What are the secrets to getting rich in a very ordinary business like plumbing or housepainting? You can find a whole tool-box full of them in Larry Harmon's story. Larry Harmon built such a phenomenal plumbing, heating, and air-conditioning service business that he made *Inc.* magazine's list of the 500 fastest-growing businesses in the United States in 1993. And his little, ordinary company in the town of Clovis, California, population barely forty thousand, topped $3.3 million in sales.

It isn't every plumbing and air-conditioning service business that conducts employee training and motivation meetings three times a week, puts the workers—called Service Advisors—through the Dale Carnegie Course, and pays them commissions and bonuses so that some are making $50,000 to $60,000 a year. That's just one of many amazing things about Larry Harmon's De-Mar Plumbing Company.

According to research paid for by De-Mar in 1988, 80 percent of the area residents thought of competitors first when they needed plumbing, heating, or air-conditioning repairs. Today, De-Mar is, by name, the first choice of a whopping 84 percent of the people surveyed! Since 1989 the company has grown 300 percent to more than $3 million in sales. And all of this despite being the most expensive service provider in the Clovis area. ''Price objections are value problems,'' says Larry Harmon. ''To win with premium prices, we must clobber competitors with service.'' And that they do. Here are the ''service advantages'' Larry used to set his company apart:

1. *Guaranteed same-day service.* Larry found that the public's number-one complaint about service people was that they never show up! So, De-Mar operates under the pressure of absolutely guaranteed same-day service. ''In our surveys, we heard the same thing over and over again,'' Larry says. ''Customers hated calling a company and being told we can get out to you in 'about three days.' They also hated the plumber not showing up at the time that was specified.''

2. *Twenty-four-hour, seven-day service without surcharges.* ''Paying people overtime is expensive,'' Larry acknowledges, ''but we make up for those costs by building our customer loyalty.''

3. *Price guarantee.* Everybody's number-two complaint about repair services was being shocked by the prices when the work was done. In response to this, Larry did something very radical; he switched from the industry norm of pricing labor by the hour, plus cost of materials with markup and travel time, with a new kind of flat-rate pricing. ''We borrowed this idea from the auto service business,'' Larry says. ''We've developed a price book that covers 98 percent of all the jobs we face. Our Service Advisors are actually tested every Monday morning on their knowledge of the price book. Then we quote the job to the customer before we begin, and that's that. If we goof and underprice a job, we live with it.''

Larry also monitors the quality of the service his people provide. *Every* customer is called after the job is completed to verify satisfaction. Employees also earn points based on praise letters and calls versus complaint letters and calls, and point totals are posted for all to see in the company's classroom. An individual can receive up to a 50 percent increase in his income, based on these points.

Every Service Advisor is actually a salesperson. When a job is completed for a new customer, the Service Advisor gives that customer a set of brochures and a plastic discount card, and explains the available option of enrolling in the company's All Season Protection Plan. And, yes, Service Advisors are paid commissions, a controversial practice that competitors claim encourages "overprescribing," but one that Larry defends passionately. When Larry switched from hourly wages to paying commissions, he paid out 21 percent more in total compensation than the prior year, but revenues jumped by 45 percent.

Not everyone can make the cut as a De-Mar Service Advisor. In a given year, nearly half of all new hires resign or are fired. There's a strict dress and personal appearance code, lots of training, long hours, and considerable peer pressure from successful SAs not to damage the company's reputation.

Larry Harmon has won recognition from excellence-guru Tom Peters, *USA Today*, and *Inc.* magazine. In 1993 De-Mar was Central California's Small Business of the Year. Larry says, "In 1985 we were going nowhere fast. When we shifted our focus to quality and service, rather than worrying about price, we became the most successful company of our kind in our area." In a six-year period, the company went from a mere $210,000 in annual sales to $3.3 million.

MILLIONAIRE-MAKER STRATEGY #15:
OTHERS MAY CRITICIZE YOU—LISTEN
TO YOUR CUSTOMERS FIRST AND MOST.

Larry Harmon's methods converted an ordinary business into an extraordinary money machine at a rapid pace, and could be used as a blueprint for transforming just about any business with a significant service component into an equally impressive success.

To sustain the company's success, growth, and reputation, 2 percent of gross earnings is reinvested in employee training, including continual additions to a company library of books, audiotapes, and videotapes, the Dale Carnegie Courses, and other seminars, classes, and special incentives. A whopping 13 percent of gross goes to advertising, including radio and television, and first-class brochures and mailings to past and present customers.

To Get Rich with an "Ordinary" Business, Try Extraordinary Marketing and Promotion

The blunt truth about most small business owners is that they are incredibly lazy, ignorant, negligent marketers. At best, the typical small business owner will have one, two, or three means of attracting customers that he relies on. At worst, he just sits there with his shingle hung out and door open, hoping for the best.

Some years ago, I did some consulting work with a spectacularly famous chiropractor who single-handedly developed not one but several million-dollar-per-year practices, one right after the other. He was nationally known for his remarkable success at attracting large numbers of new patients to his office every month—more in some months than the average doctor would gain in a year. Naturally, he was constantly asked: How do you get x number of new patients a month? How do you get thirty? Fifty? A hundred?

His answer has stuck with me ever since I first heard it. He said, "I cannot answer your question the way you want it answered, because I do not know of one way to obtain 100 new patients. But I do know of 100 ways to get one new patient, so I use every one of them."

How a New Jersey Bookstore Owner Uses "Strategic Alliances" Instead of Money to Diversify His Marketing

Roger Williams operates The Wit and Wisdom Bookstore in New Jersey, and emphasizes "strategic marketing alliances" rather than paid advertising to promote his store. He puts a catalog of current business books in the backseats of all the cars of a local limousine service. At a pizza joint down the street from the bookstore, copies of Roger's newsletter *The Reader* are stacked up and distributed free. The same newsletter is mailed to past and present customers and area merchants. When there's a movie playing at the theater in town that has a book tie-in, Roger builds a window display in his store featuring the book and promoting the movie *and* puts a display of the books in the movie theater lobby. (For example, if the film *The Pelican Brief* is playing, all of author John Grisham's books are displayed.)

How does he get all this cooperation? He asks for it! He buys tickets from the theater to use in promotions several times a year, and gives them window space at his store. The pizza shop owner uses Roger's photocopy machine free—and so on.

**MILLIONAIRE-MAKER STRATEGY #2:
DIVERSITY IS THE OPPOSITE OF LAZINESS.**

How You Can Revolutionize Any Business with "The Irresistible Offer"

I first met and interviewed Bob Stupak in 1987. He had already been "examined" by Harry Reasoner on *60 Minutes*. He had already beat a computer at poker, for a $500,000 bet, in front of 25 million people. His casino had already been visited by the rich and famous, including Frank Sinatra. And he had already irked and puzzled the powers-that-be in Las Vegas by taking a run-down slots-only parlor and, in a few short years, turning it into a 530-room, double-tower hotel and casino 100 percent debt free, paid for as he added each floor and each square foot, and running at 80 to 100 percent occupancy virtually every night. How could this be?

Since then Bob Stupak hasn't stopped. He's added a 1,000-seat showroom and another tower with 500 more rooms, and publications from the *Wall Street Journal* to *Newsweek* reported on his newest addition to Vegas World: a 1,012-foot-high "Stratosphere Tower" that, when completed, will be the tallest building in the United States and the ninth tallest building in the world. And he still keeps all 1,000 rooms filled just about every day. How does he do it?

The "secret" behind Bob Stupak's successfully slugging it out on The Strip with giant corporate competitors watching in bewilderment is: the irresistible offer.

You've probably seen Bob's full-page advertisements in *USA Today*, *Playboy*, or the Sunday newspaper supplement, *Parade* magazine. In these ads, and in hundreds of thousands of direct-mail packages sent out each year, Bob offers two nights' lodging in a deluxe room, unlimited free cocktails whether you're playing or not, champagne, free show tickets, restaurant discounts, and $1,000 of his money to gamble with—all for $396 per couple. *Yes, you read that right: You pay $396, and he starts you out gambling with $1,000.* (It is "match play," which means that on an even money bet, if you play a $5 chip of the start-up money and win, that chip is kept by the house, but you get the winnings of $5 in "real" chips. If you took all $1,000 directly to the roulette wheel, put $500 on red and $500 on black, and double zero didn't come up, you'd walk away with $500 in cash, instantly converting the $396 to $500. The reality is that Stupak starts out $104 in the hole against you, in cash. On a given day, if all 1,000 rooms are filled with these packages, he starts out $104,000 in the hole against the guests.) Most of the time, Bob even adds on to this offer with free bonuses, such as cameras, faux diamond jewelry, or Hawaiian vacation certificates.

It *is* an irresistible offer.

Actually, his only marketing challenge is making people believe it's real. When I met with him, he would not reveal exactly how many of these packages he sold per month or per year, but he did say that he runs ahead of capacity by some multiple. In other words, he sells more than the 15,000 per month he could accommodate if everybody redeemed them immediately. This means he exchanges envelopes of literature for the $396 payments months, in some cases years, before the purchasers actually make reservations and show up for redemption. It is the equivalent of having a revolving credit line of hundreds of thousands of dollars, interest free. And it is simply brilliant.

How I Personally Use the Irresistible Offer

I was so impressed by Bob's example that I am always searching for ways to incorporate the irresistible offer in other businesses and marketing situations. Frankly it's quite hard to match the appeal of his, but you can often get close. The elements you'll usually work with are: (1) creating perceived value substantially in excess of price, (2) desirable premiums, and (3) strong guarantees. The idea is to make people think, "I'd have to be dumb not to say yes to this."

In my own speaking business, I earn the lion's share of my income not from fees, but from the purchase of my how-to books and cassettes by audience members. It's not at all uncommon for me to sell $25,000 to $50,000 in materials in a six-minute "commercial" at the end of an hour-and-a-half speech. My most-used "commercial" is truly a million-dollar sales presentation; in 1994, it sold over a million dollars' worth of materials.

In that presentation, I employ all three elements to build an irresistible offer: The documented value of the materials that I offer, combined as a package, exceeds $500, but the at-seminar price is just $268; I include a collection of bonuses, including a Critique Certificate entitling the customer to submit his advertising materials to me for a personal critique; and I offer a very liberal full-year guarantee. Given that the person hearing me is interested in the subject matter and benefits of what I'm offering, he has to wrestle with the thought, "I'd have to be dumb not to say yes to this." As a result, in situations where my sales-dollars-per-person can be comparatively evaluated, I outperform most other speakers by 200 to 300 percent.

There is one caveat I should mention quickly: Your irresistible offer must be true and legitimate. There's no point in conning people. Even if you escape the legal penalties associated with such behavior, and even if you're able to sleep at night, you'll only make one-time sales; you'll never build long-term, valuable customer relationships, income stability, and financial security.

Who Says There's No Such Thing as a Free Lunch?

In chapter 5 of this book, I tell you how my client Rory Fatt turned his struggling gourmet foods home-delivery business into a huge winner with the irresistible offer. I got the idea I gave to Rory from a friend and a brilliant direct-marketing consultant, Murray Raphel, who'd used the identical strategy to create instantly a solid customer base for a new delicatessan.

Rather than build up the deli's customers slowly with costly advertising, Murray reasoned that he could take the same money and spend it all at once, up front, giving free lunches to all the potential customers who worked near the deli. Then, if the deli really delivered a great meal, the customers would return, and the business would be built almost overnight. And he wagered right.

His mailing to all the potential customers offering them a free lunch, no strings attached, no gimmicks, really, completely free, brought a flood of takers. Why wouldn't it? And the deli delivered. So the customers kept coming back and telling their friends, and the business boomed virtually from day one.

This idea is not limited to small businesses dealing with consumers, either; like all my techniques, it is adaptable to business-to-business and industrial situations, too.

I grew up in Akron, Ohio, and one of our local barons of industry was Burton D. Morgan. In a thirty-year period, Burt

Morgan started six different companies from scratch, built them up into multimillion-dollar-a-year enterprises, and sold them to or merged them with major corporations. Two of these were the largest manufacturers of specialty and "pressure-sensitive" papers in America—Fasson and Morgan Adhesives. The label stock known as "MACTAC" is Burt's best-known product. "We have a number of products which are *habit-forming*," Burt told me in a meeting years ago, "and we refer to these as our 'opium.' We discovered that the best way to sell them was to use the sales techniques used by drug peddlers: Give away lots of free samples until the customer is hooked."

Of course, this kind of marketing takes some guts. But it is a way to turn an ordinary business into an extraordinary success, in some cases, almost instantly.

**MILLIONAIRE-MAKER STRATEGY #3:
GUTSY (NOT WIMPY) MARKETING.**

How Small Can Your Beginnings Be, Anyway?

Okay, so you're not going to build a hotel or open a restaurant. In fact, you want to get started in business with a peanuts budget and somehow still make it big. How small can your start be?

Pretty small.

How about a business so small you can put the whole thing in a cart the size of two wheelbarrows? The hottest trend in the shopping mall industry these days is welcoming "temporary tenants," such as pushcart merchants. The typical pushcart merchant rents space by the month, with no long-term lease, takes up only about 100 square feet of space, sells impulse items or food items, and can get started for as little as $5,000.

Can such a dinky business make any real money? Consider The Pride of Milwaukee, started with a single pushcart by twenty-nine-year-old Kevin Callahan. The cart displayed hometown memorabilia, such as T-shirts and mugs emblazoned with Milwaukee slogans, and similar merchandise carrying the Harley-Davidson logo. In the pushcart's first year, sales topped $225,000, the next year, $308,000, with a net profit of about $80,000. The business is in its fifth year and expansion has taken the form of additional pushcarts during the holiday shopping season.

Then there's The Nutty Bavarian.

How a Nutty Idea Turned a Mild-Mannered Bean Counter into a Millionaire Entrepreneur

John Mautner was a successful accountant, earning a top salary, living in a beautiful home on the beach, financially comfortable. But he was tired of putting in twelve, even sixteen, hours a day whenever necessary with nothing extra to show for it, weary of the pressure, and restless as someone else's employee. So he threw away the security of his ten-year tenure with the accounting firm and walked away.

On more than one occasion, John had listened to his father bragging about the fresh, roasted nuts available from street vendors all over Europe. He'd done a little investigating, and concluded that—given the right locations and a hot product—pushcart vendors could make a lot of money with virtually no fixed overhead or worrisome investments in long-term store leases, store fixtures, employees, and other overhead.

Although he had no training in food preparation, John began fooling around with different nuts and condiments on his kitchen stove, with the intent of inventing a new kind of nut snack. He settled on a recipe for roasted almonds flavored with sugar, cinnamon, and several other ingredients he won't name—The Nutty Bavarian's secret sauce.

He started his business with one pushcart, at one location. No employees. Just John, his nuts, bags, a pushcart, and a hopeful smile. It goes without saying that, throughout this process, his former colleagues at the accounting firm, past clients, and friends concluded that John was nuts. His first pushcart was an instant success. People love his product. So much so that after just three years, John's company, The Sports Nut, has over fifty pushcart locations operating, many at top locations like Veterans Stadium in Philadelphia, Candlestick Park in San Francisco, the Delta Center in Salt Lake City, Universal Studios Theme Park, Kings Island, and Six Flags. In 1993 his company-owned pushcarts sold $1.4 million worth of flavored almonds, and his licensed dealers sold $1.5 million, his total sales falling just shy of $3 million.

There's also a small, but growing, mail-order business, as people discover the nuts at one of the locations, then call the company to order more. John told me they've shipped pounds of nuts to thousands of customers so far, without making any effort at all to develop this side of the business. But it's easy to see a million-dollar-plus mail-order business evolving in the near future.

How the Presidential Seal of Approval Has Helped with The Nutty Bavarian's Explosive Growth

Thanks to a chance encounter at an amusement park industry trade show, one of President Clinton's assistants got the boss's approval of The Nutty Bavarian's cinnamon almonds as the official snack of the inauguration dinners. Of course, "chance encounter" is a huge misstatement: John was doing smart, proactive things like exhibiting, distributing samples, meeting and greeting people, making things happen. The consumption of a half-ton of his snack at inauguration dinners prompted a video news release aired by local TV news programs nationwide, plus appearances on *Today* and *Good Morning America*, reaching an estimated 51 million viewers. There were also articles in magazines from *Time* to tabloids like *The National Enquirer*.

John is amazed at the number of stadium, theme park, and other facility operators who heard about him through this publicity. Some sought him out as a result. Others were eager to hear his pitch when he did contact them. As a result, he's opening new pushcart locations as quickly as he can, with a target of over 100 yet this year, 500 within three more years. He's already employing about 100 people and will probably double that with company-owned locations this year, as well as expanding by licensing to independent operators.

"I'm thirty-one years old and having a ball," John told me. "We're opening up in Hawaii next month, so I'll be spending some time there. I travel. I meet fascinating people. I got to go to the inauguration. Do you think I can build this into a $50 million company in ten years? I wouldn't mind having a $50 million corporation at age forty-one."

I don't see any reason why he can't. And John's story includes a number of Millionaire-Maker Strategies that I'll reveal as we proceed through the rest of the book. After discovering all of the strategies, you may want to come back and reread this story to see how many you can find at work.

And one thing is certain: Even from little almonds, great empires can grow!

HOW TO INVENT, FIND, OR GAIN CONTROL OF ENORMOUSLY PROFITABLE PRODUCTS

For many businesspeople, this is one of the most important "secrets" to success I think I can pass along: You must have *ownership* of at least some of the products you market, so that you have the full markup from manufactured cost to retail to work with. This is especially important for any kind of direct-marketing or mail-order business, but it applies to every business.

Why Is Control of a Product So Important?

When you buy and resell products obtained through normal distribution bureaucracies, you are going to have preset, very limited profit parameters. If you own a retail store, for example, you probably will buy just about everything from the same suppliers all the stores of your type buy from, at 40 to 50 percent off suggested retail. You'll rarely be able to sell at full retail, so you will probably have a 30 percent profit number to work with.

In the mail-order business, most vendors' normal terms will be 50 percent off in relatively small quantities, to no more than 65 percent off in huge quantities. This allows less than a one-time or 100 percent markup; however, you need a seven- to nine-times, or 700 to 900 percent, markup on your primary products to make it in direct marketing.

To bridge this gap and to make up the difference, you need

primary products that are much more profitable and you have to control them. If you have primary products with big profit markups and margins, you can have a "supporting cast" of other products with lesser markups, and still have an exceptionally profitable business.

Let's take a relatively mundane example: a chain of several swimming pool supply stores. These stores sold chlorine and other chemicals, supplies, filters and tools, some patio furniture, beach balls, toys, beverage coolers, and so on. The owner's stores were barely making money. Following a strategy of getting control of certain primary products with much higher margins, these stores went from "dogs" to big profit producers over a three-year period of time. Here's what the owner did:

1. He got his own line of "private label" chemicals (I'll discuss the private label industry later in this chapter), so instead of buying the bottled products at 50 percent off for a 100 percent markup (selling a bottle of chemicals that cost him $4.00 for $7.99), he got that same bottle for a cost of $1.00 and sold it for $6.99. This gave his business a competitive advantage in pricing, a brand-name image, and higher profits.
2. He formed a little "garage business" with teenagers "manufacturing" patio furniture out of PVC pipe, so he could advertise and sell his own patio furniture at very attractive prices. Buying normally, he might make $50 selling a set of patio furniture for $199. Now he'd sell a set for $129 and make $100.
3. He got exclusive territory rights to an automated pool cleaning gizmo imported from Korea, on which he had a 400 percent markup.
4. He put a custom T-shirt shop in each store, which is a very high-profit business if there is sufficient traffic without direct · advertising cost.

Now, he still sold everything he used to sell. He stocked several brands of chemicals other than his own, in case a customer was married to a nationally known brand. He sold the same patio furniture, beverage coolers, supplies, tools, and so on that he always had, and that customers expected to find in a pool supply store. But all those items became secondary or support products.

In the direct-marketing or mail-order business, the economics are even tougher. Almost without exception, you cannot afford to invest in advertising or direct mail to sell products with less than an 800 percent markup. As a result, just about every mail-order business, mine included, has primary products it controls, with such markups, then secondary products it also sells, but only to its "house lists" of established customers.

How Do You Gain Control of Super-Profitable Products?

There are four main ways to gain ownership or exclusive control of a product:

1. Create
2. Publish
3. Secure certain exclusive rights
4. Have it private-labeled for you

Create Your Million-Dollar Product from Scratch

Behind every famous—and not-so-famous—product there's somebody who had an idea and the gumption to do something with it. Who knows how many people have played charades? Rob Angel added a playing board and cards and came up with Pictionary. Burt Reynolds and the late Bert Convy also created a game based on drawing out charades and moved it from the living room to TV, where *Win, Lose or Draw* was a successful game show for years. The next time you enjoy a Popsicle, you can thank Frank Epperson: Way back in the winter of 1923, he left a glass with a spoon in it on a windowsill and watched the

Popsicle invent itself. Then he patented it. PerfectSmile, marketed by my client, the Guthy-Renker Corporation, was invented by a dentist.

But for every one of these inventors who has the thrill of seeing their product become a big star, there are thousands more who toil in relative anonymity, but can still quietly make fortunes. Wilson Call is in that category.

In 1987 Wilson Call, an architect by training, first got the idea for a small fused adapter to go on a TV set plug, to prevent fires in case of shorts. It so happens that this was and still is a huge problem; in fact, many experts insist that the number-one cause of home fires is the TV set's cord. Convinced of the need for such a device, Wilson worked on it and ultimately perfected and patented the Fireplug TV Cord Protector.

"I thought, like a lot of other potential inventors, that all I had to do was get my patent," Wilson recalls, "then when the patent was issued I would contact various firms through the mail, show them my product, they would purchase the patent from me for cash and royalties, and I would sit back a rich man, to dream up some other device and repeat the process.

"Little did I realize how amateurish that idea was. In no time at all I found out that this was not the case. To have an idea and bring that idea to a point where a patent can be filed is a complex matter. If you really carry the idea through in a manner that if you were to manufacture and market the device on your own, would it succeed? In most cases, that is what you are going to have to do."

Wilson's rude awakening *does* parallel that of most inventors. He had to take the product to the marketplace himself, working through a maze of manufacturers, assemblers, packagers, legal requirements, and distribution problems, eventually investing nearly $200,000 before getting the first Fireplug onto the first retail store shelf.

I'll be the first to tell you that I admire inventors like Wilson. But I've never had any desire to be one. The fastest way to *lose* a million dollars is to be an inventor.

This is a very tough road. That's why it's quite easy to use Methods #2 and #3: The landscape is littered with inventors and manufacturers sitting on products they've poured heart, soul, and all the money they could beg or borrow into, but can't sell, and have no earthly idea how to sell. If you are going to create from scratch, my very best advice is to create to fit a known, identified, affordably reachable target market or to supply an established distribution pipeline. In other words, create it only if you know how you will market it and that you can market it. And, for safest results, work backward: Have the market and marketing in place first, then invent.

If we break down the ideal market, *known* means that the market exists, can be described, and that you either know a lot about it from personal experience or a lot of information about it is available through reference materials, periodicals, shows, or other sources. *Identified* means that others have already done the work of profiling this market and proving certain theories about it. For example, "fishing enthusiasts" is an identified market; from magazine subscriber databases and specialty catalog companies' databases, we can easily get a feel for the size of the market and its makeup in terms of men, women, ages, income levels, and purchasing behaviors, all from research sources available at the public library.

Affordably reachable is very important. This means that your prospective customers all read one or several magazines, are all available on mailing lists you can rent, all go to a big event where you can exhibit, all watch a particular TV program, etc. In contrast, if you define your market only as American women, it will cost millions to reach them, because you must use a lot of costly mass media; you'll have to advertise on daytime and nighttime television, in dozens of magazines and newspapers, and you'll be fighting for their attention with giant advertisers like Revlon, Procter & Gamble, and General Mills. Women who own or fly private aircraft is an affordably reachable market. There will be one or two magazines they all subscribe to and read. They will attend air shows. A mailing list will be available.

You can best justify inventing, creating, or finding products and organizing a business around them when you match up with this type of market.

For example, the operators of Good Sam Club, which provides various services and publications to about 300,000 RV owners, who "live the RV lifestyle," are just getting into the business of assembling their own catalog of products of interest to RV owners. Although they will mostly assemble, catalog, and sell existent products, they certainly can afford to invest in inventing and developing some of their own, new, exclusive products, based on input from their members, because they are virtually certain of being able to market those products successfully. The risks of inventing are dramatically reduced; the problems of finding distribution nonexistent. Obviously, these situations exist for established companies, not for start-up entrepreneurs.

If you are determined to be a from-scratch inventor, I'd encourage you to get a copy of Wilson Call's how-to manual, *The Anatomy of an Invention* (see chapter 13).

An Inside Look at the Tough Challenge of Inventing from Scratch and Turning That into a Profitable Business

If you are thinking of going the invent-from-scratch route, an honest appraisal of the obstacles ahead of you is important, which brings us to Tom Doyle, a consulting client of mine with a big problem. Tom invented a product so different from its competitors that it requires educating consumers to sell it, but it's so low in price that there's no way to cover the costs of a lot of educational-type advertising like infomercials or direct-mail campaigns.

Frustrated with how quickly his hand and arm fatigued while playing tennis, Tom Doyle became obsessed with grips. Yes, grips. And grip designs haven't changed much in 1,000 years. So Tom went to medical school libraries, visited with experts in the anatomy, anthropology, and physiology departments of five universities, analyzed pro athletes' gripping problems, molded clay in his kitchen, and, over a five-year period, filled his garage with different prototypes. In 1988 his ultimate, revolutionary Endurance grip design was granted Patent Number 4,736,950, and his company, Gripping Solutions, was born.

At the urging of a friend, he first applied his design to creating new handlebar grips for mountain bikes, and the product is acknowledged by championship mountain bikers, mountain-bike product retailers, and doctors as far superior to anything else on the market. Yet, sales are so slow that Tom and his wife still run the company single-handedly, go to gatherings of mountain-bike riders to demo and sell them personally, take orders, pack and ship boxes, and still can't seem to set aside any money for advertising or developing additional products.

Through Tom's almost annoying insistence at telling anybody and everybody about his grip technology, he wound up convincing a buyer for the Smith & Hawken gardening tools catalog, who happened to buy a mountain-bike grip, to order grips made for several of Smith & Hawken's most popular tools. So, Gripping Solutions will be in a Smith & Hawken catalog soon, and although it has been a financial hardship for Tom to do the redesign work to apply his design to those specific tools, this could be a big breakthrough.

There's no doubt in Tom's mind that he can develop golf club grips that will improve anybody's game, tennis racket grips that will improve anybody's game, industrial product grips that will improve safety and reduce repetitive-motion injuries, and, well, the applications are endless. But the funds aren't.

In 1994, Gripping Solutions, Inc., stacked up only $164,000 in sales and lost about $20,000 doing it. In spite of ringing endorsements from just about every bicycling magazine, the Endurance products do not race off store racks—they are priced higher than other grips by necessity, and, so far, nobody's found a way to get the package or in-store displays to tell enough of Tom's story to sell the item. Until recently, the product was judged as too inexpensive and too price-competitive to permit marketing direct to the consumer, but, at my urging, a price increase and packaging of two pairs together as a set is being done, so that a reasonable attempt can be made at marketing direct to bicyclists by direct-mail and direct-response print ads.

Time will tell whether my advice is good or bad. I'd call it a 50-50 shot.

Tom is now aggressively seeking venture capital through exclusive licensing and joint ventures—for example, trying to find a golf products company that might invest in his company or give him R&D money in exchange for exclusive use of the technology for grips for their golf clubs. And he is wrestling with the possibilities of going to friends, relatives, neighbors, maybe even customers and dealers to sell stock in the company, but he is fearful of giving up equity and control. But the time Tom can devote to this mission is limited—he also has to sell enough grips to keep the doors open and the lights on. And even spending the money to get on an airplane and go to a candidate company's offices for a meeting or to a trade show is a seriously debated, agonizing decision.

Tom's struggle is the story of the inventor. Reading this, Wilson Call will empathize instantly. And if you are going to go down this path, be prepared for this sort of struggle. It's not for the weak of heart.

However, should Tom tough it out and solve his marketing problem in the bicycling industry, that alone might yield million-dollar profits over two or three years. A deal to supply a major manufacturer or marketer of golf clubs might be worth hundreds of thousands of dollars a year, maybe even more. Success in the Smith & Hawken catalog could lead to distribution of various kinds of grips through hundreds of other catalogs, and provide a million dollars or more a year in profits. All that can happen —if Tom can tough it out.

MILLIONAIRE-MAKER STRATEGY #23:
IF YOU'RE GOING TO INVENT,
CONSIDER MARKETS FIRST.

In retrospect, Tom Doyle feels—correctly, in my opinion— he would have been much better off perfecting, manufacturing, and marketing grips for golf clubs, tennis rackets, or even fishing poles before mountain bikes, based on the size and responsiveness of the markets. Had he carefully researched and analyzed these markets and chosen one to be first on an objective basis, his business would be much further along than it is.

An Invention Story with a Very Happy Ending Full of Millionaire-Maker Strategies

On a warm, sunny autumn day in 1985 in the small town of Sharon, Pennsylvania, James Winner walked out the door of his office building, eager to get into his prized Cadillac—equipped, incidentally, with a factory-installed security system—and enjoy the ride home after a tough day at work. Unfortunately, there was an empty parking space where his Cadillac had been. Right in front of his own business, a thief had bypassed the Cadillac's alarm system and stolen it!

That's how Jim Winner got the idea for a now-famous product, THE CLUB. He brought THE CLUB to the market in 1986 and only eight years later, THE CLUB has become a $100-million-a-year company. The now-famous CLUB, brilliant in its simplicity, clamps to any car's steering wheel and makes it impossible to pilot the car. Getting it off requires more time and effort than most car thieves are willing to invest, so they pass a car with the bright-colored CLUB fastened to its steering wheel and move on to an easier target. Jim's company guarantees up to $500 against the car owner's insurance deductible if a vehicle is stolen while protected by THE CLUB and, in 1992, received theft claims for less than one-sixteenth of 1 percent of the 3.1 million CLUBs that had been sold up until that time.

Recently, Jim's been busy marketing additional security products, notably including THE DOOR CLUB, for homes, which received the 1993 Retailer's Choice Award from *Do-It-Yourself Retailing Magazine*.

> **MILLIONAIRE-MAKER STRATEGY #5:**
> **TURN ANGER AND RESENTMENT AGAINST**
> **AN ENEMY INTO ENORMOUS OPPORTUNITY.**

Who says "crime doesn't pay"? Jim Winner's personal experience with the very frustrating crime of auto theft sent him in a very profitable direction. People everywhere are increasingly frustrated with auto theft and home burglary, worried about their personal and family safety, and angry at the criminal element in their communities. With auto theft on the rise, Jim Winner stepped forward with an easily understood, easily used, affordable, and credible solution.

Incidentally, the entire anti-crime industry is booming, so Jim Winner is riding a wave. Sales of Mace, the leading self-defense spray, jumped 36% from 1991 to 1993. Quorum, a newcomer to security products, using an Amway-like multilevel marketing system with independent distributors, has gone from 10 million in sales in 1991 to well over 100 million in 1993. All this puzzles some business analysts, because, overall, crime is not, statistically, getting worse. However, the public feels unsafe, and is trying to buy a safe environment.

| MILLIONAIRE-MAKER STRATEGY #4: KEEP IT SIMPLE. |

In an increasingly high-tech, complicated world, there's tremendous opportunity in going against the grain with a low-tech, simple solution to important needs or desires. There's certainly nothing high-tech about Jim Winner's CLUB, but it works.

| MILLIONAIRE-MAKER STRATEGY #7: PROVIDE THE CUSTOMER WITH AN EXCEPTIONAL GUARANTEE. |

"Satisfaction guaranteed" may be an overused phrase, and some marketing experts will argue that point, but I believe the American consumer so frequently has the experience of spending money on products and services that fail to live up to their promises, that he is more responsive than ever to a particularly bold, clear, and specific guarantee. For years, in my seminars on marketing, I pointed to the original Domino's guarantee as an example of how an entire business can be built on one bold, specific promise (fresh, hot pizza delivered in thirty minutes or less).

With THE CLUB, you are guaranteed payment of up to $500 of your insurance deductible if your car is stolen while protected by the device. As a marketer, I'm going to tell you a couple of the "tricks" of that guarantee. First of all, a lot of people who buy THE CLUB or get it as a gift never use it. How many, still in their unwrapped packages, are sitting in car trunks or corners of garages? There's no way to know, but my bet is it's in the tens of thousands or more. Second, some people are going to forget about that guarantee as time passes between their purchase of the device and a theft incident a year or years later. These and similar facts of human behavior diminish this company's apparent financial risk attached to this guarantee left and right. So this strong guarantee, like most strong guarantees, is not nearly as risky or costly as it might seem on the surface.

Then, as a business manager, I'd speculate that this cost is factored into the selling price and "reserved" to pay these claims. At the very beginning, Jim Winner had to guess, had to have great faith in his product, and had to stick his neck out making this guarantee. But soon, as a consistent, and in this case very small, percentage of claims became known, the company need only add the cost of claims to the product and reserve that portion of sales to be perfectly safe. (If THE CLUB is a $50 item on average, 100 of them represents $5,000 at retail, approximately $2,500 in wholesale revenue to the company. Suppose the claims are one-sixteenth of 1 percent. One-sixteenth of 1 percent of $5,000 is $3, divided by 100 units, which is a whopping *3 cents* per unit!)

For the price of three cents per unit, Jim Winner gets a super-strength guarantee he can brag about in all his advertising, on his product packaging, and in retail displays. And, think about this: The person who does have a car stolen and obtains that $500 from THE CLUB tells everybody he knows what a fantastic company this is and how they honor their guarantee.

This is good business—good for the customer, very good for the company.

How to Print All the Money You Want, Legally!

Here's my personal favorite: paper-and-ink, audio and video "information products." With these types of products, you can create or license or get exclusive rights or private label, you can manufacture as needed (publish on demand), and you can enjoy huge profit markups. I've devoted all of chapter 9 to this lucrative area of opportunity.

Securing Certain Exclusive Rights Is Almost as Good as Inventing—Heck, Maybe Better

Why would a manufacturer give you exclusive rights to a product, especially without requiring you to put up any money?

To many people's surprise, this happens all the time, and is perfectly logical. Let's assume you are a manufacturer of costume jewelry wristwatches. Your company makes all kinds of different watches: men's, women's, kids', watches with sports-related faces, watches that are look-alikes of very expensive watches, and so on, and you supply discount-store and drugstore chains like Wal-Mart, Kmart, Target, Gold Circle, and Walgreen with these watches. That's your business.

Along comes a guy who says he understands the freestanding kiosk business, is starting a company to put people in shopping centers with freestanding vendor carts or kiosks, wants to use your watches as one of the inventory packages and product lines, and needs exclusive rights to this type of distribution. And he presents himself in a professional and businesslike manner. He asks for a one-year exclusive limited to that type of distribution, renewable annually for five years only as long as he buys at least 100,000 watches the first year and at least 200,000 watches each year thereafter. He's not asking for credit, or for you to do anything special. He'll pay cash with orders, and you'll drop-ship watches in assortments of 500, reorders no less than 50, to his locations all over the country. Well, why *wouldn't* you do this?

If the guy is honest and succeeds, you're going to sell 900,000 watches, more or less, over the next five years, *in a way you have never sold watches before*. If he fails, you're still going to sell some number of watches less than 100,000 but in the thousands the first year, *in a way you've never sold watches before. And you had and have no intention of selling watches that way on your own.* So, although the exclusive has plenty of value to that guy, it has no value to you. You're giving up something that costs you nothing and has no value to you, with the possibility of getting a whole new distribution network in return. You have the proverbial nothing-to-lose-everything-to-gain situation. Marketers using this very argument carve out exclusives for themselves with tens of thousands of manufacturers every year. This is sometimes called the "Cossman Method," after E. Joseph Cossman.

Joe Cossman is one of the few early pioneers of the mail-order business who specialized in securing exclusive mail-order rights to products already being sold via other means, then exploiting them through direct marketing and publicity. I met Joe when I arranged an infomercial deal for him, and I helped him create an updated version of one aspect of his famous home study course for sale on television.

Let me tell you a little bit about one of Joe's twenty successes: Fly Cake. One Sunday, Joe was reading the classifieds in the newspaper—one of many techniques he's used to find interesting products—and he spotted a little ad that read:

**Send in $1.00 and
we'll send you Fly Cake.
It kills flies.**

So he sent in a dollar and got the product. It was a doughnut-shaped, solid cake of chemicals that seemed to attract flies, and killed them on contact. When Joe contacted the inventor, he learned that during World War II the inventor had been in the army and had been given an assignment to find an effective insecticide for the South Pacific. The sprays being used didn't work and were costly, so he came up with this solid cake that lasted up to a year. After the war, he set up a little factory and, for twenty years, made Fly Cake and sold it only through classified advertisements in newspapers and magazines. In total, he'd sold about 300,000 Fly Cakes.

Joe said, "Give me the exclusive rights for this product and I'll sell a million a year, or I'll give you back everything I've done with it and it won't cost you a cent." Joe and the inventor reached an agreement, exempting classified advertising, but otherwise giving Joe exclusive marketing rights for Fly Cake. "At that moment," Joe told me with enthusiasm, "it was as if I had invented the product and owned the factory!"

Joe sold Fly Cake in an incredible variety of ways. Within three years, he'd sold over *8 million* Fly Cakes. He subsequently sold the business and his rights. Fly Cake alone made Joe more than a millionaire.

> **MILLIONAIRE-MAKER STRATEGY #26:**
> **IF YOU DON'T ASK, YOU CAN'T GET.**

Don't assume you can't secure exclusive rights to a desired product or that manufacturers won't work with you because you're too small or any other limiting belief. There are enough actual obstacles to overcome without manufacturing more of them in your own imagination. The only way to know for sure how any individual or group of people will respond is to make your best possible argument, under the best possible circumstances.

How to Make Your Fortune with "Private Label" Products

The private label industry is, to me, one of the most interesting and appealing places to go for products on earth.

For some years, I had an interest in a small network marketing company, and at peak we had nearly 100 products under our label. By all appearances and perceptions, they were "our products," yet they were standard or stock formulas being made by a private label manufacturer for a number of different companies. The only difference between ours and dozens of other companies' was our product names and labels and our identity.

For example, we found the manufacturer of a truly superb aerosol weed killer. This stuff got to the roots and killed just about any weed on contact. You could spray a weed in a sidewalk crack, come back ten minutes later, sweep away a little brown residue, and that was that. This company produced tens of thousands of cans of this product, labeled one way for a national chemical company that sold exclusively to restaurants and hotels, labeled another way for a national hardware chain that sold it off the shelf. When we first added the product to our line, we piggybacked on those runs and bought plain white cans, just 144 at a time, and labeled them with our own printed paper labels. When our purchase size increased tenfold, we switched to having the manufacturer silk-screen imprint our label on the cans for us. The product bore our proprietary name ("Kills Weeds Dead"), our label, our company name.

This same manufacturer provided us with a terrific insecticide spray that smelled like pink bubble gum, a foam leather cleaner, and a waterless car polish. We also dealt with private label manufacturers of cosmetics and skin-care products, vitamins, herbal formulas, weight-loss drink mixes, even CS-gas keyring spray containers used to ward off attackers, competitive with the Mace units you now see sold in stores.

While working on this project, I got a real education in the private label business. The truth is that you can get just about any product made or sold anywhere manufactured and private-labeled for you, in surprisingly small quantities. Every industry has private label manufacturers, and they are easy to find because they tend to aggressively advertise in their industry's trade magazines and exhibit at their industry's trade shows. In the beginning, if you are starting out with small quantities and stock, standard formulations, there will be little or no negotiation—the manufacturer will have a price list. There are virtually no pitfalls. Most private label manufacturers even provide blanket product liability insurance that extends protection to your company. As you move into volume purchasing, you can negotiate prices, extended payment terms, and having your company added as a full coinsured to the manufacturer's product liability insurance, at the manufacturer's cost.

The bottom-line is that it is remarkably easy, pleasant, and profitable to deal with most private label manufacturers. If you have a clever marketing or promotion plan, a means of distribution, a chain of stores, maybe even one store, a catalog, or a celebrity who'll work with you to promote a particular type of product, you can probably have your own product or product line without research and development costs, without starting from scratch, and without having to invest in huge quantities by dealing with private label manufacturers.

Where Do You Go to Find Products, Product Sources, and Product and Business Ideas?

Product and business ideas really are everywhere. All around you. But there are some specific sources that can be of help to you:

1. Trade journals*
2. Trade associations*
3. Conventions, exhibitions, trade shows, and consumer shows*
4. County and state fairs, swap meets
5. Catalogs
6. Consumer magazines
7. "Opportunity" magazines
8. Government publications
9. Directories*
10. Classifieds
11. Old advertising
12. Import/export*
13. Current events
14. Trends

* See chapter 13 for more information.

You Can Also Advertise for Products and Product Ideas and Let Them Come to You

Some years ago, a friend of mine in the business of brokering products to the mail-order industry ran this ad in a major city newspaper:

Millionaire consultant seeks inventors, manufacturers, importers, authors, etc., with unique products suitable for promotion to homeowners, do-it-yourselfers, gardeners, and hobbyists. Send your information in confidence to:

He ran this ad one time, on a Sunday, in the Business Section, in a two-inch box. How many replies do you think he got?
280.
If you ran a comparable ad in a handful of magazines or newspapers or in *USA Today*, you'd probably be deluged.

How Do You Pick a Winner?

For most people, the most efficient approach is to first lock in on a market and a product category. This allows you to focus your energies and resources.

The best way to pick your product category is to consider your own educational and vocational experience; your own interests; the subjects and activities you know a lot about already; the size, responsiveness, and reachability of different markets; and societal and economic trends. You'll need to use a combination of these to do the best job possible.

You should also keep in mind that most highly promotable products, services, or businesses have at least one of these three ingredients:

1. They solve an almost universal need and problem. The air conditioner is a great example of this type of product, and since its invention and early marketing, home and car air conditioners have moved from the luxury to the (perceived) necessity category. When the microwave oven was first manufactured it was assumed it would have only a limited market in the restaurant industry. But societal changes that made time such a precious commodity, and made fixing the evening meal fast a perceived necessity, provided the right environment for the microwave to become a universally accepted and desired household appliance.

2. They provide a much better way to perform a common task or do a common, necessary job. Just about every kitchen gadget is sold with this theme. The ballpoint pen, the calculator, and the fax machine all fall into this category. Positioning an in-home fitness device against the costly, cumbersome task of going to the gym incorporates this idea into a marketing message. The self-sealing strip added onto plastic sandwich bags is this type of invention.

3. They have some enormous emotional or impulse appeal that transcends logic and basic needs. "Snob appeal" products, the fanciest restaurant in town, and cosmetic products all fit into this category.

Having a Mental, Emotional, and Experiential Link with Your Market Can Make You Rich

A guy at one of my seminars said, "I just saw that 'Flying Lure' infomercial on TV, I read about how much money they're making, and I'm going to find a fishing gizmo and do the same thing."

"Do you fish?" I asked. This guy didn't fish; in fact, he had never even gone fishing once, didn't have any friends who did; heck, he'd never even heard of *Field and Stream* magazine. And he was about to dive in and have to swim upstream against some very tough currents. And probably drown.

The people I respect most in the outbound telemarketing business, Steve Pittendrigh and his team at InfoCision, feel so strongly about this ''link'' issue that when they're making calls to sell golf products to previous buyers of golf products, they hire and staff the phones with telemarketers who play golf on their days off. When they're making calls to solicit donations for a particular charity, they use telemarketers who are very sympathetic to the cause or philosophy of that charity. Why? Because a golfer knows another golfer when he hears one. Nothing you can do in a sales script can match the power of shared passion.

Picking a market you are suited to exploit first and then going after salable products is a smart approach.

> **MILLIONAIRE-MAKER STRATEGY #20:**
> **EVERYBODY HAS ASSETS OF EXPERIENCE AND**
> **EMPATHY THAT SHOULD BE CONSIDERED**
> **AND VALUED WHEN CHOOSING**
> **BUSINESS ACTIVITIES.**

4

HOW TO "REINVENT"
YOUR WAY TO A FORTUNE

How would you like to have been the guy who invented the microwave oven? Or came up with Kleenex? Or 7UP? Or Dixie Cups? Or the Timex watch? Hey, you'd be in Fat City now, wouldn't you!

Maybe. Maybe not.

In their first incarnations, every one of these products was a dead-bang *loser*. In his book, *Getting It Right the Second Time Around*, Michael Gershman tells the stories of these and other famous products that failed when first introduced to the marketplace. In one way or another, they were "reinvented" before becoming successful. And there are fortunes to be had by clever entrepreneurs who creatively reinvent products, services, even entire businesses that are almost right.

There Are as Many Ways to Reinvent as the Imagination Can Conceive— Plus One or Two More

Our homes, closets, refrigerators, garages, and offices are full of products that had to be reinvented to succeed:

• Timex watches went from failure to success when all conventional distribution channels for watches, such as jewelry stores, were abandoned, and the low-price, incredibly durable watches were put on sale in—horror of horrors—pharmacies.

- Dixie Cups were originally just a component part of a cumbersome water fountain no one would buy.
- For the first six years of its existence, Kimberly-Clark did everything that could be thought of to sell Kleenex as a superior makeup removal product. When they finally got around to checking up on the few customers that were buying the product, they discovered people were using it to blow their noses, not to take off makeup. The advertising was changed accordingly and sales boomed.
- 7UP, originally called Bib-Label Lemon Lime Soda, was marketed as a means of settling infants' upset stomachs. Later, as 7UP, it was positioned as an adult hangover remedy. This product struggled for survival all the way into the 1960s, when the "UNCOLA" ad campaigns caught on.

If you are sitting with a product you passionately believe in but have been unable to market, you have to start by giving yourself an attitude checkup. You start by getting past blaming the stupid, unresponsive public, so you can make changes to the product that the public will respond to. The individual who brings an idea to the marketplace and gets hammered naturally prefers speculating about the idiocy of the public rather than looking in the mirror, shoving his bloodied nose aside, and squinting through his blackened eyes to look at the guy who missed the mark.

"Everybody needs this product. How can they not see that?" I've listened to countless thoroughly frustrated clients and would-be clients stuck on this thought. Then he'll be off on a long celebration of how great his product is and what a genius he is, followed by a tirade about how dumb the customers are. I've heard it at least 1,000 times. I confess, I've muttered it myself a few times. But if you can set disappointment, frustration, and ego aside and, with fresh eyes, find ways to reinvent, you can turn losers into winners. That's the ThighMaster story.

So You Thought ThighMaster Was an Overnight Success? Think Again.

Just how famous is ThighMaster? Murphy Brown got one at her baby shower. President Bush once joked that Marvin Fitzwater had busted his. Jay Leno jokes about it. Phil Donahue came out on stage wearing one on his head. The thing shows up in the darndest places. And millions of them have been sold.

But this product was initially a turkey.

In case you've been living in a cave, ThighMaster is a doohickey for women to put between their legs and exercise with to firm up their thighs. It has two blue foam-covered loops connected by a spring hidden inside a red plastic ball. It is pitched on television, in print ads, and on its box by Suzanne Somers, best remembered as the ditzy blonde on the sitcom *Three's Company*, a forty-five-year-old with the fantastic legs of a dancer half her age—the living, walking, prancing proof that ThighMaster works wonders.

Last year, when I spoke as a member of a panel at the international convention of the Direct Marketing Association (DMA), I got the inside story of this product's failure from one of my fellow panelists, Michael Clark, vice president of Ovations, Inc., the company that reinvented ThighMaster and produced its first successful TV commercials. Originally a Swedish import invented by medical people, ThighMaster was given a dull, technical-sounding name, and, after the inventors' own attempts at TV advertising, was a failure. Here are the three changes that turned ThighMaster from a loser into an enormous winner:

1. *Product appearance.* The original version was, well, ugly. The spring in the middle that creates the tension was visible, and looked like something you'd see under the hood of your car. And there was no mystique—it was just two loops hooked to a spring. Big deal.

   Reinvented, it has bright blue foam covering its loops and,

most importantly, the spring has been concealed inside a fire-engine red plastic ball, now called "the hidden tension coil." The whole thing looks sort of space-agey.

2. *Positioning.* The original version was designed and presented as a multipurpose exercise device. And, in the first commercials, women were shown in exercise leotards, in a workout environment, exercising with the thing. At my DMA panel, Michael Clark said, "We decided that the person watching the TV commercial, sitting on the couch, might not be all that excited about leaving the couch and really *working* at this."

Their new approach showed the device being used by Suzanne Somers and others while sitting in a chair watching television, lying on a chaise lounge next to a swimming pool, and sitting in a comfortable chair, talking on the phone. The message: This isn't exercise at all! And, to keep the message from being confused, they zeroed in on just one purpose—firming up the thighs—and changed the name to match.

3. *Celebrity.* A celebrity spokesperson was sought out who would really use and benefit from the product, get involved in the business, and, as Michael put it, "go the distance"—not only appear in advertising, but put her image on the package, go to in-store appearances, create publicity, do interviews, and in every way marry the product.

The person who signed on was Suzanne Somers, who tells anybody who'll listen that she uses her ThighMaster two or three times a day, carries one in her purse, takes it with her when she travels, and recommends it to friends. In an appearance on *The Maury Povich Show*, she gave one to every member of the audience and they all sat there and Thigh-Mastered together while she answered questions.

"There's no doubt that Suzanne put this product over the top," Michael told me, "but even she couldn't have made the original version a hit without the other changes made to the product."

Roughly one out of every twenty-five homes has a ThighMaster in its closet, and the product continues to sell successfully both via direct-response advertising and in retail stores, thanks to this clever reinvention.

This success may—and probably should—pique your interest in obtaining a celebrity spokesperson for your product, service, or business. On a national level, many celebrities are found and obtained for entrepreneurs by professional celebrity brokers listed in chapter 13. You can also contact the celebrities or their agents directly, as a result of your own research with the Academy of Motion Picture Arts Directories (see chapter 13). For local businesses, locally popular athletes or TV or radio personalities can be just as effective as a much costlier national celebrity, and in most cases, you can contact these people directly.

The costs for celebrities vary widely, depending on your product, whether you're going to use the celebrity in print advertising, direct-mail, or broadcast media nationally or regionally, whether they are spokespersons or actually personally endorsing the product, and other factors. It's not as expensive as most people think, though. Significant national celebrities can be obtained for national campaigns for as little as $10,000 to $25,000 a year, often plus a royalty tied to resulting sales.

MILLIONAIRE-MAKER STRATEGY #45:
IT AIN'T OVER 'TIL IT'S OVER.

Do You Remember That Goofy Cat-Face Clock with the Eyes and Tail That Move Together?

Woody Young, a friend of mine, has spoken at my seminars, and may be one of the most unusual entrepreneurs I know. Woody, who lectures on both business and Christian life topics, has owned and operated a successful plant nursery and written children's books. Somehow, along the way, he stumbled into and bought the California Clock Company, makers of the famous Kit-Kat Clock.

Famous? Yes, famous. In the fifties and early sixties, you'd see one of these things on a kitchen or rec room wall in millions of American homes. Maybe you'll remember having one in yours. It's fifteen inches from ear to tail tip, black and white, with big bulging eyes, a big smile, bow tie, clock in its stomach, and a long tail. The eyes and tail move together, tick, tock, tick, tock. Classic kitsch.

Woody saw the Kat as something more. "It really is a unique item. Very few novelty products stay in perpetual manufacture and distribution for fifty years. There's something special about it. It makes even the worst sourpuss smile. Even the toughest customer'll look at it and say 'Look at that dumb clock,' but that's the worst reaction it gets." So, he bought a small clock company and diversified its business in incredible ways.

For starters, he created the Kit-Cat Fan Club, and began enrolling members with inserts inside each clock package. He created the Kit-Cat Creed: "Put a smile on everyone's face, love in everyone's heart, energy in everyone's body and be a positive force in everyone's life." There's a monthly Club newsletter, puzzles, games, stories of the magic the Cat and the Creed have worked in people's lives. There are tens of thousands of members. And, of course, there are Kit-Cat posters, T-shirts, bumper stickers, coffee mugs, cookie jars, aprons, and the Kit-Cat Wristwatch. He has even licensed the Kit-Cat character, just like Disney licenses Mickey Mouse. If you visit the famous Ron-Jon Surf Shop in Daytona Beach, Florida, you'll find the Kit-Cat on their surfer apparel, even on a surfboard.

Next, he turned the Kit-Cat into a personality for how-to books. There's *Clockwise Quotes on Life*, a motivation book; *Babysitting Wise*, in which Kit-Cat gives practical instructions for baby-sitters and parents; *Clockwise*, which teaches children how to tell time; and *Song Wise*, which illustrates patriotic songs.

Woody still goes personally to gift industry trade shows, dressed in a Kit-Cat-like tuxedo and bow tie, with a Kit-Cat-like smile, to show and sell his smile-inducing products. But he also has a national salesforce calling on all kinds of stores and distribution through many mail-order catalogs, including *Wireless*, the catalog of esoteric merchandise put out by Minnesota Public Radio.

The company's value has increased nearly twenty times since

Woody bought it, literally on a whim, with a flash of inspiration about the untapped value of Kit-Cat, and went on to reinvent the entire business.

If You Ain't the Lead Dog, the View Never Changes

One of the principles espoused by advertising gurus Al Ries and Jack Trout, authors of *Positioning: The Battle for Your Mind,* is: If you can't be first in a category, set up a new category that you can be first in.

In the early 1980s, the chiropractic profession was deluged with "practice management firms," each offering high-priced services via multiyear contracts, and all promoting their services with free, introductory seminars. I did some speaking for several of these companies, studied their businesses, and saw that while the profession was clearly crying out for help with marketing their practices, many doctors couldn't or wouldn't invest $20,000 to $50,000 in a services contract, so they came to the introductory seminars but went home empty-handed and unsatisfied. A collection of elements came together through a process I won't bore you with that led to my developing the same kind of how-to information, but packaging it for sale at a very modest price (under $1,000) to the doctors in books, manuals, audiocassettes, and do-it-yourself kits. So a business was born.

But I didn't want it to be just another business in a cluttered field. Somehow, I wanted it to be the "lead dog" from the very beginning. After some thought, my partner at the time and I made these decisions:

1. Because we delivered all of our advice in the form of materials rather than through services, we could call ourselves *publishers*.
2. Because we were using introductory seminars, we could also call ourselves a *seminar company*.
3. Because we were teaching generic practice marketing strate-

gies, we could *mix professions* rather than being profession-specific. After a little testing and experimentation, we found that mixing chiropractors and dentists in the same seminars worked best. We were the only company to do this.

Combining these three elements, our company *instantly* became "*the* largest integrated seminar and publishing organization exclusively serving the chiropractic and dental professions," because we were the *only* company doing that. We invented a new category.

By the way, none of the three people in this company was a doctor. We were all outsiders, marketing and businesspeople translating success principles to these professions.

Our business grew like wildfire and, in a period of just several years, did millions of dollars in business in a very small niche market, reaching out to fewer than 60,000 potential customers. Within chiropractic, the more responsive of the two markets, we achieved a 30 percent market share. I am convinced our creation of a new category, where we could advertise ourselves as the biggest and the best from the very beginning, played a major role in the professions' acceptance of us as valid experts.

How Domino's Became the "Lead Dog"

The Domino's Pizza story has been told so many times, you may think there's nothing more to be said. But I think Tom Monaghan's reinvention of the pizza shop deserves mention here. I interviewed Tom Monaghan for a magazine article, and he emphasized that early in the development of Domino's, he recognized the critical need to position his business in the minds of consumers as different from other pizza places. "We tried to find something about the pizza business no one else was doing well," Tom said. That was delivery.

If you keep reinvention in mind, you can see that Domino's actually set up a whole new category within the pizza business: delivery only. And Domino's became such a success, the lead dog in this category, that the longer-established, bigger Pizza Hut

tried ardently to buy Domino's before settling for entering the
category as a Johnny-come-lately competitor.

MILLIONAIRE-MAKER STRATEGY #16:
TWEAK, TWEAK, TWEAK.

Often, success is just one or two minor adjustments away.
Many people give up just one "tweak" away from turning experimentation and struggle into victory. But how do you draw
the line between persistence and stupid stubbornness? In most
direct-marketing situations, if a marketing test returns less than
sixty cents in gross sales per dollar of marketing expense, we
walk away. If it's sixty-one cents or better, it can often be
tweaked to profitability. In each situation, you have to somehow
decide whether or not you are close enough to keep investing in
tweaking.

If Edison had given up easily, I'd be writing this book in a
room lit by a candle!

MILLIONAIRE-MAKER STRATEGY #37:
TAKE FULL RESPONSIBILITY FOR THE SUCCESS
OR FAILURE OF YOUR IDEAS.

Blaming the marketplace, the customers, those in charge of
distribution for not seeing how great and wonderful and needed
your product is cannot possibly lead to success. It may be com-
forting, but it's self-defeating. It's even childish, like saying "if
you won't play my way, I'll take my ball and go home." If the
inventors and advocates behind ThighMaster had gotten mad at
their market and gone home, it'd be just one more failed invention among thousands of fitness devices that also failed. Instead,
they kept seeking different and better ways to present their product in a way that the public would respond to.

MILLIONAIRE-MAKER STRATEGY #38:
SUCCESS BREEDS SUCCESS.

Woody Young took a simple, odd, but successful product and turned his imagination loose on it—how can we build on this success?

The process of getting to success with a product can be long, agonizing, and costly. Once you get there, though, you should take fast, massive, and comprehensive action to capitalize on that success in every way imaginable.

As soon as my client the Guthy-Renker Corporation had a hit with Vanna White on television selling the PerfectSmile tooth-whitening products, the race was on to create Perfect-Smile toothbrushes and mouthwash, PerfectTan, PerfectSkin, and PerfectWhatever, to build on the foundation of success.

> **MILLIONAIRE-MAKER STRATEGY #8:**
> **STAKE OUT A LEADERSHIP POSITION.**

There's great value in being perceived by your marketplace as the biggest and/or the best, as the leader of your field. You can get to that point the hard way: starting at the bottom and crawling, fighting, clawing your way up the ladder, over a period of years, slowly building a reputation. Or you can, as Robert Ringer put it in his great book *Winning Through Intimidation*, "leapfrog" to the top. You can leapfrog by reinventing your entire business or the entire industry your business is a part of, or by inventing a whole new category within that industry.

How Do You Take on Nabisco, Del Monte, Kellogg, and Other Big Brand Names and Win?

There are two battles to be fought in the foods business: one for supermarket shelf space, the other for the attention of the fickle consumer. David A. Nichols came to Loblaws, a Canadian supermarket chain that was losing money, and concocted a radical idea about getting rich. He proposed taking Loblaws's lackluster group of private label foods, improving their quality, and aggressively marketing them to other supermarket chains for their use as their private label brand. In other words, Nichols wanted to fight for shelf space and sales with the big names. And he wanted to export to the United States to boot!

David Nichols saw three opportunities. First, he found that most private label lines of food were of inferior quality or at least perceived to be of inferior quality to the name brands, so only the most budget-conscious consumers reluctantly bought them. He believed he could change that. The quality of private label items could be dramatically enhanced and still sell for less than the big names because they carried no "brand tax." In other words, their prices did not need to include the tens of millions of dollars that the big names spend each year on advertising.

Second, he noticed that most supermarket chains' private label products were packaged almost in plain brown wrappers. They looked uninviting and cheap. Nichols determined that in volume, snazzy packaging was no costlier than dull packaging. So he put his "President's Choice" products in packages with copy that sells, like their "Ancient Grains" cereal, boldly labeled across its top: "Too Good To Be True!" And in the newspaper inserts he develops and provides for promoting his products, you'll see things like an elephant standing in a stewpot and the instruction "Cut elephant into bite size pieces. This should take approximately 2 months" to advertise President's Choice deep-dish meat pies. He gave personality to products that historically have been put forward with none.

Third, he had his own testing lab in Loblaws stores. If he could quickly prove the salability of these products, he would be exporting more than just another product line to U.S. supermarkets, he'd be offering a proven sales system, a franchise of sorts. In a sense, he completely reinvented the private label foods business and created something of much greater value to offer to retailers throughout North America.

Nichols's "Way-Out Ideas" Pay Off—
to the Tune of 9 Billion Dollars!

The results have been phenomenal. President's Choice foods have been adopted by over 1,200 stores throughout the United

States, including chains like Lucky Stores on the West Coast, Jewel in the Midwest, and D'Agostinos in New York. According to the *New York Times*, while overall North American supermarket products' sales volume rose by 37 percent in 1993, President's Choice sales jumped 127 percent. When Nichols came to Loblaws, its private label food sales were $500 million. After three years, they've topped $9 billion! And some individual President's Choice products, such as the "Decadent Chocolate Chip Cookies" outsell major brands like Chips Ahoy. Loblaws also private-labels its products for Wal-Mart.

Competitors have been awakened by David Nichols's achievements. Major chains like Safeway and A&P have revamped their own private label lines, now Safeway Select and A&P Masters' Choice. David Nichols says that "retailer-created and -controlled brands" may account for as much as 40 percent of the supermarket industry's food products sales in the near future.

Nichols has already tired of this game that he created, has left Loblaws, and has begun a consulting business; he is talking about building a new wine distribution business around his small family winery. Aspects of his strategy are well worth considering for a variety of businesses.

MILLIONAIRE-MAKER STRATEGY #25:
UNCOVER HIDDEN ASSETS AND OPPORTUNITIES.

For example, the small businessperson who is trying to find a way to get really, really rich might learn from Nichols's exploits. Let's say you own a small chain of restaurants or hair styling salons or carpet cleaning trucks. If you develop your own private label line of ancillary products and a terrific system for selling them, you can then roll that out to others in your business all over the country and create *an instant, nationwide sales and distribution organization* for your products. Nichols turned a neglected, undervalued product line into a new, very duplicatable system not unlike a franchise, although not called or sold as a franchise.

In concert with this idea, we might summarize Nichols's attack as delivering comparable or superior quality at substantially lower prices by operating with a minimalist advertising budget. By riding on others' established distribution networks, stores, store traffic, and advertising, he was free to concentrate on innovation with product and product packaging. Or, for example, it's worth noting that David Nichols saw great opportunity in an asset that was "lying around" at Loblaws, undervalued, neglected, and taken for granted by those who had controlled it for years. That very same situation—what I call the "hidden opportunity" in an established business—exists just about everywhere. Or, for example, take note that David Nichols ignored conventional industry wisdom, norms, rules, and traditions when he chose to build on private label products, rather than offering them as an "oh, by the way" accommodation to "cheap" customers. There are lots of lessons to be learned from the story of President's Choice.

Dan Kennedy's Creativity Checklist for Inventing or Reinventing Products, Businesses, and Marketing Messages

Here's a little checklist I refer to whenever I work on a brand-new product or on re-invention:

OPPOSITES   The Burger King Whopper is a big sandwich; the White Castle Burger is a very small burger, often sold in six-packs and dozens. Is there something that is successful and big that could be successful and small or vice versa? Today's common indirect lighting was invented as the opposite of the traditional, standard direct lighting. As I mentioned elsewhere in this book, 7UP was made by its positioning as "The UNCOLA."

**MAGNIFY/
MINIMIZE**

Consider the foot-long hot dog, the mini-van, the big-screen TV, the pocket-sized TV, single-serving puddings.

ADAPTATION

If it works in one business, will it work in mine? The drive-in window has moved from banks to fast-food restaurants to all sorts of applications: quick-print shops, dry cleaners, liquor stores. In Las Vegas, the Imperial Palace Hotel & Casino has a drive-in window for sports bettors to place wagers on baseball, football, basketball, and horse races without leaving their cars.

**EXAGGERA-
TION**

Years ago, Volkswagen demonstrated the "roominess" of its car by having basket-ball star Wilt Chamberlain get in it and sit comfortably. Even though no one really believed that Wilt would regularly drive a Bug, the point was made: If he can sit in it, it's certainly big enough for me. Varia-tions of that idea have been used in dozens of car and minivan commercials. My friend and client Frank Robinson has driven the sales of millions of jars of Nancy Kwan's Pearl Cream by having her deliver this guarantee in TV commercials: "If your friends don't actually accuse you of having had a face-lift, return the unused portion for a full refund." This is nothing more (or less) than a satisfaction guarantee, but it has much more impact by being said with exaggeration—no one really believes they'll be accused of having had a face-lift after using Pearl Cream, but they say to themselves, "If they say it's that good, maybe it'll make these laugh lines go away."

ADDITION/ SUBTRACTION

Lite and fat-free foods are products sold based on what has been *subtracted* from them. At one time, there were two kinds of doughnuts: cake and glazed, both round, with a hole in the middle. Eliminating the hole and filling them changed the doughnut business forever. The next time you visit a Dunkin' Donuts take a look at how many varieties are "filled"—creme-filled, jelly-filled, lemon meringue–filled, maple syrup–filled, chocolate-filled. That's *addition*.

COMBINING

One odd type of business that has cropped up in recent years is the combined Laundromat–Tavern: Singles do their laundry, enjoy a beer, watch a game, and make friends all at the same time. But a much more common example is the combined supermarket–gas station—the convenience store. How about the clock-radio? The hit TV series *Miami Vice* was a creative combination of cop shows and music videos.

REARRANGING   I have no idea who is credited with having invented it, but the calzone, an Italian treat, is a pizza turned inside out. Theater-in-the-round is an immensely popular rearrangement of the "normal" audience and stage setup.

GENERAL PURPOSE VS. SPECIAL PURPOSE   The now-giant Amway Corporation was launched with a single product called "L.O.C.," an abbreviation for Liquid Organic Concentrate, which was initially pitched as the replacement for dozens of household products cluttering up your closets.

One company in the home-cleaning product field I've worked with briefly has a different specialty product for every imaginable purpose: There is a grease-based stain remover, a water-based stain remover, a carpet stain remover, a pet stain remover, an ink stain remover, and on and on. The truth is that 80 percent of the products are 99 percent the same; the most significant differences are their names and labels.

TIME FRAMES

Some years ago, a hugely successful weight-loss product promotion was "Burns Off Body Fat, Hour by Hour." Today, Slim-Fast has a very successful ad campaign based on the theme "Give Us a Week and We'll Take Off the Weight." Tom Monaghan built his Domino's empire in a saturated business with "in 30 minutes or less." The "Weekend Getaway" was invented as a means of promoting hotel stays by locals.

PACKAGING THAT SELLS

Certainly for products that must sell off the shelf, packaging is a critical concern. A fantastic package that has done its job for 100 years is the Animal Crackers box: a circus train car with cage bars, and the cookies shaped like circus animals visible inside the cage. For years, Pez candy was popular because of the dispenser package. Right now, Duracell is heavily promoting its package that includes its own battery tester.

SPECIFIC SOLUTIONS

Waterproof, wear-proof, tear-proof mascara and lipstick are bestselling cosmetics. The pet door lets your dog go in and out of the house at will without you letting him in and out, and without compromising your home security.

COINED TERMINOLOGY

Ad genius David Ogilvy came up with "Schweppervescence" for Schweppes tonic water. To describe the unique marketing strategies I teach, I coined the term "magnetic marketing"—attracting qualified prospects or customers rather than pursuing them.

SYMBOLS

Think of some of the most enduring symbols: the Pillsbury Dough Boy, Betty Crocker, Ronald McDonald, the NBC peacock. In the TV infomercial business, Mike Levey brilliantly developed a "franchise" with his Amazing Discoveries format, used for one infomercial after another.

TECHNOLOGY

How can you jazz up your business, service, or product with technology? In one of my businesses—the publishing of how-to materials—the staple has been audiocassettes plus written manuals, but, increasingly, software diskettes are being added to these products. *Entrepreneur* magazine, for example, now includes a diskette with many of its famous business start-up manuals. Restaurants accept take-out orders by fax.

5

HOW PROVIDING A SERVICE CAN MAKE YOU A MILLIONAIRE

When most people think of "service businesses," they automatically think small. The solo operator who comes around and cleans your carpets. The guy who cuts your grass. But the service industry is booming, with many giant businesses as members.

How an Unemployed Autoworker Invented a Revolutionary Approach to Advertising in His Garage

A young, unemployed autoworker, Terry Loebel, was looking for a way to make some money when he stumbled onto an idea that would ultimately change the entire advertising industry. With nothing but time on his hands, Terry was hanging out, talking to some of the shopkeepers in town, and the complaint he heard repeated over and over again had to do with the difficulties and high costs of advertising to attract new customers. Terry figured out that he could reduce each merchant's costs if they all mailed their brochures and coupons together, sharing one envelope. He convinced several merchants to try his idea, borrowed $500 from his mother to finance the printing costs, and stuffed the envelopes himself, in his garage.

In 1993 the business he created celebrated its twenty-fifth

birthday in a big way: Val-Pak mailed more than 250 million envelopes filled with different advertisers' coupons to more than 50 million homes throughout the United States and Canada. These days, dry cleaners, carpet cleaners, restaurants, stores, chiropractors, dentists, attorneys, and countless other types of local businesses as well as national advertisers rank Val-Pak as their best method of advertising. The company has over 250 dealers and an army of more than 1,000 salespeople, bringing in advertising from more than 80,000 businesses, resulting in nearly 6 billion coupons delivered to consumers.

Val-Pak is the largest and fastest-growing company in the industry invented by Terry Loebel. Others now nipping at its heels include MoneyMailer and Advo. By providing a simple, cost-saving service to small businesses, the company Terry created in his garage with $500 has become a $70 million-a-year business.

I Can't Wait to Tell You About Rory Fatt

Inspired by Domino's Pizza and trends he read about in Faith Popcorn's book *The Popcorn Report*, a young entrepreneur in Vancouver, Canada, started Simple Salmon, home delivery of fresh-frozen seafood and gourmet dinners. His is a pure service business, competing against "calling Domino's and settling for a pizza," going out to eat, or going to the supermarket and assembling a dinner. Rory's product is convenience without compromise of quality.

He started his business in his apartment, with a small corner of borrowed freezer space at a vendor's facility, and one 8½ × 11" flyer. When he came to my seminar, he was struggling just to stay in business, and he said to me, "Once I get somebody to try my meals, they *all* reorder, stock their fridge, and keep calling me for more. If I can just get somebody to try it, I keep them as a customer."

I said, *"If you're telling me the truth, I have the solution to your marketing problem. If you're lying, my advice will put you out of business."*

We reinvented Rory's entire marketing campaign around the concept of a free dinner. My advice was: Give it away and get 'em hooked. And he did. Using the theme "Who said there's no such thing as a free dinner?" he launched ads in the Yellow Pages, weekly newspapers, and on radio, and gave away free dinners by the carload. Since then, he's used a variety of innovative advertisements but, in every case, he sticks with the free dinner offer as the means of acquiring new customers.

In every sense, we have conquered Rory's marketing challenge. He can acquire new customers at a very low percustomer advertising and promotion cost, and his retention and referral rates are outstanding. Because he started with zero capital in the first place and still can't convince any bank to make a sizable business loan to such a strange enterprise, he is, as I'm writing this book, wrestling with other business problems: raising capital so he can maintain adequate inventories, employ people, open pick-up outlets, and expand before someone bigger and better financed takes his idea and preempts him in the marketplace. If he gets over this hump, I believe Rory has an eminently franchiseable business and you may very well see his ads in your city soon. His dramatic success to date is based on many things I believe in devoutly, including selling quality, not price; competing with service above all else; and using direct-response, creative advertising featuring an irresistible offer.

The trends that fuel his business can fuel many, by the way. The most precious commodity of the 1990s is not money, gold, silver, or diamonds—it's time. That's what we have the least of; that's what we'll cheerfully pay to preserve. With both husband and wife working outside the home; kids to raise; homes to keep up; a new interest in health and fitness motivating use of gyms, walking, jogging; an endless variety of leisure activities; and a remarkably large percentage of people between the ages of twenty-five and fifty involved with spare-time, home-based businesses, there's just not a minute to spare. So people will spend money for convenience. If you can give people time, you can make a fortune.

How to Build a Multimillion-Dollar Business Without Spending Even a Penny on Advertising

For years, requests by viewers of TV programs for transcripts of the shows were a damned nuisance until James Smith recognized the opportunity hidden in all that aggravation. Smith was an MIT dropout, operating a small typesetting business in Manhattan when he ordered a transcript of a *MacNeil-Lehrer Report* show and waited three weeks for it to arrive. To demonstrate that even his dinky company could do a better job, he taped a *MacNeil-Lehrer* show, stayed up all night transcribing and typesetting it, and hand-delivered the product to the show's producers the next morning. He secured an exclusive contract to produce the show transcripts and fulfill the requests.

For TV producers, his oddball business, called Journal Graphics, offered a service that relieved them of problems. Smith said to the producers: You can flash the Journal Graphics address and phone number on the air, we'll handle the requests, and if a particular transcript sells enough copies, we'll even pay you a royalty. He quickly captured the transcript rights to most major talk shows and about one-third of all of CNN's programming.

Of course, most shows do not generate enough transcript requests to amount to much money. But, then, keep in mind that the costs of preparing a typical transcript for copying are less than $100, and copying costs are about two cents a page, about a buck for the average complete transcript copy. Journal Graphics lays a 300 percent or better markup on that, selling each transcript for $3 to $5. And the occasional blockbuster bestsellers make it all worthwhile. Phil Donahue's April 8, 1993, show, featuring the "Recipe Detective's" do-it-at-home versions of Reese's Peanut Butter Cups, Kentucky Fried Chicken, and other famous food products sold 100,000 transcripts! Bill Moyers's PBS interviews with Joseph Campbell about myths sold a respectable 20,000 transcripts.

It all adds up to over $3 million a year, with an advertising budget of zero. And the business is on a growth curve. In addition to the individual consumers interested in the Recipe Detective or the interviews with transvestite hookers who want to adopt children, Sally Jessy Raphael, law firms, newspapers, radio talk show producers, and even government agencies want transcripts of all the *Nightline* programs, and they'll pay extra for fast delivery via satellite, computer, or fax. For $1,000 a year, Smith will deliver transcripts from 100 different TV shows whenever they deal with your chosen subject, so if you are, say, a lobbyist for the travel industry, you can get the comments about the travel industry as they occur on these shows. *In these cases, Smith is really in a double-service business:* serving the broadcasters and producers of the shows and serving the user of the information.

To use high-tech terms, you might think of Mr. Smith's Journal Graphics as a toll booth on the information highway. But it is solidly based on the simple foundation of all successful service businesses: the ability to do and deliver a desired and needed service for less money than the individual customers can do it themselves, faster and more conveniently than they can do it for themselves.

MILLIONAIRE-MAKER STRATEGY #6: SELL TIME.

Make a Million with Your Hobby!

How do you choose a service business to start? If you have an interest in creating a highly promotable service, but no ideas for that service, take a fresh look at your own hobbies and personal interests.

Quite a few "success experts" emphasize the idea of doing those things you enjoy so much that you would do them for free as the most likely path to financial success. For me that would narrow it down to sleeping, eating, and hanging out at the track, and I haven't yet found a way to put those activities together into a high-paying business. But I do agree that it is infinitely easier to stick with something you are passionately interested in long enough to get rich, than to set out just to get rich in whatever seems like the best opportunity of the moment. And many people can and should look to their hobbies and personal interests as the source of inspiration for making their first million.

How an Idea for Decorating a Living Room Wall Turned into a Unique Service Business

In 1964 Micheline Massé, a University of Montreal commerce graduate, began collecting old stock certificates with the intent of papering a wall in her living room with the colorful, often beautifully engraved documents. All of the certificates she found, bought for pennies, or got from friends were presumably worthless, but before gluing them all up, she decided to research a few of them and make sure they were worthless. And darn the luck, one of the old certificates had a value of $5,000. That screwed up her decorating plan, but it also launched Micheline in a new business as a stock sleuth.

On the Trail of Lost Fortunes!

According to Micheline, about 2,500 companies change their names every year, mergers and reorganizations confuse stockholders, bankruptcies often disburse funds years later, dormant companies' stockholders give up, and people die, leaving stock certificates in trunks in the attic or shoeboxes in the closet that go unnoticed for years and when found are presumed worthless. All this adds up. In fact, she estimates the amount of available, "lost" wealth to be in the billions of dollars, and that one-third of all households have some seemingly worthless stock certificates lying around.

Just as an example, consider North European Oil Corporation, a "penny stock" from the 1930s. The company shut down in 1937. But twenty years later, oil was discovered on its properties, the company was reactivated under a new name, and original stocks suddenly had value. For every $100 worth of that stock from 1930, there's $130,000 waiting today. And there are nearly a million of those shares still floating around out there, presumed worthless by whoever has them.

Florence Richards, a retiree in St. Petersburg, Florida, bought 300 shares of North European at twenty-five cents a share in 1930 to cheer up a despondent, failing stockbroker she was dating at the time. Florence read about Micheline; Micheline got her $54,500 in back dividends and capital growth for those 300 shares!

Remember the famous capers of Bernie Cornfeld and Robert Vesco from the 1960s? If you do, you may remember their "Fund of Funds," which ended with a much-publicized scandal, Vesco's disappearance, Cornfeld's prosecution, and the fund's bankruptcy. Well, it took thirteen years to settle the bankruptcy, and now hundreds of millions of dollars await fundholders and shareholders who file claims.

30 Percent of Millions Recovered—Micheline's Hobby-Turned-Service Becomes Big Business

The company Micheline founded, StockSearch International, Inc., has an extensive database in its computers, a network of research associates all around the world, and a crew of investigative specialists, all tracking down the true value of old and obscure companies' stock certificates. The company charges a small, flat fee for each investigation (under $100 as of this writing), plus 30 percent of the recovered funds if the stock proves valuable.

And even if the stock is really worthless, the certificates may still be salable in the collectibles market. Micheline's original hobby lives on, as she remains active as a dealer in collectible stock certificates. Over the years, she has recovered millions of dollars for her clients. And she finally found enough truly worthless certificates to get that wall decorated!

Where Might Your Interests Lead You?

My friend Carl Galetti is passionately interested in direct-response advertising and copywriting, and comes to many of the direct-marketing and advertising conferences where marketing gurus speak. He listens as one speaker after another, at conference after conference, recommends certain books to the audiences by the old masters of advertising, many of which are out of print. Classic books like *The Robert Collier Letter Book*, originally published in 1931, and *Scientific Advertising* by advertising pioneer Claude Hopkins are incredibly valuable to anybody interested in creating highly productive ad copy, but these books are almost impossible to find.

Carl correctly saw this as a terrific opportunity. He dug up many of these old books, traced them to their copyright owners, negotiated new publishing deals, and published new editions. In some cases, he found inventories lying in dusty warehouses and tied up the rights to sell them. In other cases, he arranged drop-shipping agreements with little-known publishers. One way or another, Carl built up a catalog of nearly a hundred of these hard-to-find but recommended books. Now, just about every direct-marketing and advertising speaker refers their audiences and clients to Carl. There are at least fifty speakers I know who tell people about Carl. By providing an important service to people interested in learning marketing from the old masters *and* providing a service to today's marketing teachers, Carl has built a profitable mail-order business with zero advertising.

But why stop there? Remember, Carl loves going to all sorts of marketing conferences and hanging out with the speakers, consultants, experts, and entrepreneurs who gather there. So, using his books as the foundation, Carl assembled a speech and a home-study correspondence course of his own on the old masters' copywriting techniques. Now Carl goes to the conferences as an invited speaker, a recognized expert, and with catalogs to distribute and courses to sell, so instead of spending thousands traveling to each conference, he makes thousands at each one.

> ### MILLIONAIRE-MAKER STRATEGY #10:
> ### EVEN IF YOURS ISN'T A TRUE SERVICE BUSINESS,
> ### ADD AND EMPHASIZE A SERVICE COMPONENT.

Carl's book business is a mail-order business, but by positioning himself as the provider of the service of tracking down and providing these difficult-to-find, rare, or out-of-print books, he built his mail-order business without a cent of advertising.

Earl Nightingale once observed, "If, instead of working on making more money, the average businessperson would spend an hour each and every day in quiet contemplation of how to be of greater and more creative service to his clientele, he and they would be the richer for it."

A Related Moneymaking Secret Is to Go
Where Your Talent Takes You

I started in speaking, as many do, giving talks and seminars on self-improvement, motivation, and general success subjects. And I took just about any and every speaking opportunity that came along. "Can you speak about the mating habits of the New Zealand bumbarabbit?" Certainly. It just so happens that last month, a client of mine in the bumbarabbit breeding business . . .

You can get good at speaking that way. I did. And you can make a living that way. I did, and many do. But my speaking income and the demand for my services really took off as I moved further away from those common, universal topics and, instead, focused on speaking about marketing and direct-marketing strategies and systems, where my greatest talent is, and where my greatest interest is. For me, devising the right marketing strategies for different products, services, or businesses, and teaching people how to select and use the best strategies for their purposes, is not only easy, it's fun. I'd rather do this than play golf, to the constant consternation of my wife. The line between work and play is blurred.

When that line is blurred for you, I think you've found the

right track to your fortune. Of course, some dose of reality has to be added to the mix; you need a place where the line blurs, but also where there is a sizable, responsive market for the end result of your energies and efforts.

> **MILLIONAIRE-MAKER STRATEGY #21:**
> **TURN YOUR PASSIONS INTO PROFITS.**

The entrepreneurial path is, at best, a very rocky one, with landmarks like long hours, frustration, fear, financial worries and woes, and, quite literally, one obstacle placed in front of you after another. If you are going to have the persistence necessary to travel very far on this path, it'll help to be involved in an activity that genuinely interests you and stirs your passion. It is much easier to make a million dollars doing something you enjoy and are excited about for its own sake than to make a million purely to make a million.

FOUNDATIONS FOR A SUCCESSFUL SERVICE BUSINESS

1. Need-driven (examples: oil change shop, computer repair)
2. Want-driven (examples: interior decorating, portrait photography)
3. Time savings–driven (examples: mobile oil change, lawn and garden service)
4. Money savings–driven (example: furniture re-covering and reupholstering)
5. Unique or incorporating a strong competitive advantage (example: 1-Hour-by-appointment appliance repair: We set a definite appointment and guarantee to arrive within one hour of the appointment time or your repair is free.)
6. Linked to personal interest, preferably a passion
7. Linked to a personal talent, ability, or specialized knowledge

---

HOW THE AMAZING POWER OF DUPLICATION TURNS EVEN SIMPLE IDEAS INTO IMPRESSIVE FORTUNES

This premise is simple: Create a means of making money, building and operating a business, or something similar that has unique features and can be taught to and duplicated by others, and then charge others for the privilege of using your "system."

Yes, I've just described McDonald's and virtually the entire franchise industry. But there are a number of other, less complicated, costly, regulated ways of getting paid for others' use of your proven system. So, after just a few words about franchising, we'll move on to more interesting opportunities.

Franchising Just Ain't What It Used to Be, but It Still Might Be Your Million-Dollar Opportunity

In its earlier years, franchising was a way for the little guy to get into business for relatively little investment and minimal risk, thanks to the proven system, training, and continuing support of the parent company, the franchisor. Over the years, franchise fees and start-up costs have gone through the roof. These days, many of the very best franchises are not sold to first-time business owners at all; they are sold to established, successful franchisees in another franchise network. McDonald's franchisees own Domino's franchises, Dunkin' Donuts franchises, Alphagraphics franchises, etc., and the entire industry has become somewhat incestuous.

Of course, if you do have a business right and ripe for franchising, you may still find your fast fortune as a franchisor. As a starting point, you might obtain some information from the International Franchise Association in Washington, D.C. However, just the cost of getting ready to sell your first franchise, notably including legal fees and complex, costly federal and state registrations, can be prohibitive. In response to the increasing costs and complexity of becoming a franchisor, and the related high costs and barriers to entry for ordinary folks as franchisees, new, different, innovative, and simpler formats for putting people in business have come to the forefront, and it is these that I want to focus on in this chapter.

Could You Get Rich Selling a Business in a Box?

Consider my clients and friends, Len and Sandy Shykind, their company, U.S. Gold Chain Manufacturing, and its main business, "Gold By The Inch." An inveterate entrepreneur, Len Shykind had been in over twenty different businesses, some modestly successful, some gut-wrenching disappointments, when he got the idea for Gold By The Inch. The idea is a simple one: Display gold chain in different patterns on spools, uncut; let the customer choose the pattern; cut the chain to the exact length for her wrist, neck, or ankle; and then add the hoop ring and clasp, providing made-to-order jewelry instantly, on the spot. The first Gold By The Inch display was a clunky, homemade unit, which Len and Sandy, kids in tow, schlepped out to swap meets and to a location in front of a buddy's gift shop to test Len's idea.

From the first day of selling, at an outdoor swap meet in Phoenix in July, in just six months, working only on weekends, Len and Sandy personally sold over $40,000 of Gold By The Inch. And, incidentally, the markup in this product category is enormous. Comparable chains in jewelry, department, and even discount stores typically carry markups of fifteen to twenty times, so Gold By The Inch Dealers mark their products up eight to ten times (800 to 1,000 percent) and still offer customers bargains! With $40,000 in sales and nearly $30,000 in profits in six months from a part-time business, Len and Sandy realized they had a duplicatable, marketable business opportunity that other people would be thrilled to have access to.

From a Tabletop in a Swap Meet to a Growing, Global Business

Eleven years later, Len's company, U.S. Gold, has started nearly 10,000 Gold By The Inch distributors in business throughout the United States, Canada, Australia, New Zealand, England, Africa, Arabia, Greece, and Japan. Most have part-time or spare-time businesses. Many take their portable business to swap meets, fairs, and bazaars, some sublet space from host stores in malls and shopping centers, and a few operate kiosks or carts. All together, U.S. Gold distributors sold over $25 million at retail in 1994.

The product line has expanded to include a wide variety of rings manufactured in U.S. Gold's own factory, even imported pearls, but still the entire "jewelry store" requires only a tabletop of space and relies on the shiny, beckoning spools of gold chain to attract customers. People can get started in the business for as little as $399, although the average new Dealer starts with about $1,000 worth of inventory at cost. It's not uncommon for a Dealer to turn that entire inventory over in just a couple of weekends, and be back for more.

Thar's Gold in the Simplicity of This Business

The fortune that Len has made in just ten years is largely thanks to the appealing simplicity of this business. Len says that the key to the success of his business could be copied by many others. "People understand the product, its appeal, and how the business works instantly. It's easy to do and the product just about sells itself, so just about anybody can see themselves doing it successfully. And the high markup means that only a few sales a day can still put a couple hundred dollars—maybe $30 or $40 an hour—into the Dealer's pocket." Len created a successful business-in-a-box *anybody* can do, anywhere, anytime.

How Television Created Quantum-Leap Growth for U.S. Gold

For years, U.S. Gold recruited almost all of its new distributors from advertisements in national magazines like *Moneymaking Opportunities, Income Opportunities,* and *Entrepreneur,* but the company's big breakthrough came with its first TV infomercial. With a simply and inexpensively made half-hour TV program describing Gold By The Inch, with interviews with Len, Sandy, successful Dealers, and industry experts, the number of people requesting information about getting into the Gold By The Inch business skyrocketed, and the advertising costs of attracting those people actually dropped. The infomercial I produced for U.S. Gold has now set a record as the longest continuously airing lead generation infomercial for a business opportunity. It has aired almost every week on national cable networks like Discovery and The Family Channel and hundreds of local stations in cities and towns throughout the United States for over five years.

At the time that we put together and started airing this infomercial, there were no other lead generation infomercials of its kind. We pioneered a new approach, since copied successfully by others. The infomercial has been directly responsible for millions of dollars of sales, quantum-leap growth in the Dealer or-

ganization, even a surprising amount of brand-name recognition
for the company and its jewelry. The infomercial was even spotted by an executive at the huge MGM Grand Hotel and Theme
Park in Las Vegas, which has led to the first Gold By The Inch
permanent location store, The Gold Mine, in the MGM Grand
Theme Park. The store is managed by Len and Sandy's son, who
worked his way through college selling Gold By The Inch at
swap meets. His store should easily sell more than $500,000 of
Gold By The Inch in its first year.

The Booming Business of Business Start-up
Boot Camps

As the prices of franchises climbed out of many people's
reach, a number of entrepreneurs came forward to fill that gap
with business start-up seminars, often marketed as "boot camps."
Essentially, the participant receives the same training and education he would get if buying a franchise, usually in a five- to
seven-day crash course, but then he is turned loose to start his
own independent business based on what he has learned. He's
provided with a system of doing business, but no continuing
parent-company relationship.

One of the pioneers and leaders in this field is Laurence J.
Pino, an attorney by training, an entrepreneur by experience, and,
in recent years, a teacher by preference. Over a twenty-year period, Larry started and operated thirty-five different businesses,
created and marketed The Desktop Lawyer software program,
and has spoken to over 300,000 people in seminars in 125 different cities. Along the way, he founded The Open University,
based in Orlando, Florida, a stone's throw from one of the ultimate monuments to entrepreneurial guts and glory: Disney
World and Epcot.

The Open University currently sponsors start-up boot camps
for two different types of white-collar businesses: the mortgage
aftermarket business, discounting, buying, and brokering real estate mortgages, and the commercial factoring business, matching

business owners eager to convert receivables to fast cash with specialized lenders and investors who buy or lend against receivables.

Each boot camp lasts a full week, and costs about $7,000 per person—a fat price for a seminar, but a cheap price for being put into a business. The camps are all conducted in Orlando by a team of Open University instructors, outside speakers who are successful in the businesses being taught, Larry Pino himself, and supplemented with reference manuals, audiocassettes, and videotapes.

Most students learn about the two business opportunities by attending free or low-cost preview seminars put on in fifty to seventy cities a year by a traveling team of Open University instructors and enrollment representatives. In Orlando, there's a team of "student counselors" who talk with potential but unconvinced students by phone, answer their questions, help them with financing, and, overall, are responsible for two-thirds of the enrollment activity.

"I decided to use my experience and contacts to find and select only the most exciting, unusual, little-known, and exceptionally profitable home-based businesses," Larry explains, "and then assemble formal, standardized, quality training in every detail of starting and operating that business, on par with a mini-MBA and with a franchise. American colleges and universities provide very good information, but it's not always practical or clear how to use it in a practical way in the real world. When I thought about forming a comparable institution of higher education, I wanted to make sure it would teach people how to become successful in their lives, and be accessible to just about anybody. That's what we've done."

Essentially, The Open University has two different, proven A-to-Z businesses that it has made easily learnable and duplicatable by most people, and that is the asset they leverage, to the tune of millions of dollars a year. Larry Pino is certainly not alone in this approach. A quick flip through all the advertising in a current issue of *Entrepreneur* magazine, for example, will reveal over fifty different companies using this same nonfranchise, crash-course approach with an incredible variety of businesses, from the operation of retail clothing stores or travel agencies to becoming a home inspector for new home purchasers or a property tax reduction advocate for businesses.

Network Marketing Is Another Way to Profit from the Power of Duplication

The granddaddy of this often misunderstood, sometimes mocked, but nonetheless giant industry is the Amway Corporation. Started in 1959 by two boyhood friends, Rich DeVos and Jay Van Andel, with a single product, an all-purpose cleaning liquid, the Amway Corporation has grown into a billion-dollar-a-year empire distributing hundreds of its own products; a secondary catalog of brand-name merchandise, including clothing and appliances; MCI discount long-distance; and other services through a network of independent, mostly spare-time distributors radiating from the small-town home base of Ada, Michigan, to literally every nook and cranny of the world. In the process, it has endured a lengthy battle with the Federal Trade Commission over representations of its compensation plan and earnings promises made to would-be distributors, and ultimately become the standard of stability and integrity for a very volatile industry. It has also made its founders, along with many distributors, very, very rich. A few years ago, at the beginning of his retirement from Amway, Rich DeVos cheerfully plunked down the price to buy the NBA team the Orlando Magic without blinking an eye. But it's instructive to look underneath all this to the very foundation of Amway's success through duplication.

The Amway empire is based on a few profoundly basic premises. First, simple products anybody can understand, use personally, tell friends about, and easily demonstrate and that, in many cases, everybody uses, so the distributor need not ask a customer to buy something new, revolutionary, or unnecessary, only to switch sources for products already regularly purchased and consumed. This made the retail side of the business duplicatable by anybody, even if they lacked even a semblance of sales aptitude.

Second, the adherence, almost exclusively, to word-of-mouth marketing, so that the monies customarily spent by household products, cosmetics, food, and service corporations on expensive mass media advertising could be redirected and used to generously compensate the independent distributors.

Third, the idea that each distributor would earn some money from selling products to consumers at retail, but make the big money through duplication, by showing another person how to get into the business, sell products, and duplicate all over again. Amway calls this process "sponsoring," because it has many similarities to sponsoring someone in a 12-step recovery program, fraternal club, or association. A relatively complex structure of "overrides," tracked by a massive computer system, provides each distributor with compensation based on the activity of each person he personally sponsors, and each person those people sponsor, virtually ad infinitum. The idea is that each distributor learns a set of simple skills, then duplicates those skills in each person he sponsors. When such a structure is subverted in one way or another, most commonly with a practice called "inventory loading," it crosses the legal line from legitimate network marketing to an illegal pyramid scheme. There are subtle but important differences.

How Gary Haiser Married Multilevel Marketing to an Offbeat Collection of Business Ideas

There are always new, young, ambitious network-marketing companies starting up, but most fail for a variety of reasons. As of this writing, of 1,800 known network-marketing companies in America, fewer than 20 have survived for five years or longer. One of those is led by Gary Haiser, who considers himself a new breed of network marketing entrepreneur.

Gary is building his own multilevel marketing (MLM) company. His company, Personal Wealth Systems, Inc., is following a relatively conservative growth plan, marketing goods, services, and monthly dues-driven memberships, all with the stated mission of helping ambitious Americans live debt-free. Last year, its ninth year in business, PWS's sales doubled from the previous year's, topping $5 million.

Gary Haiser's first career was in the music business, as a studio musician in Detroit's Motown community, playing backup drums for some of the biggest names in the music world. While working as a studio drummer and playing club gigs, he started a home-remodeling business, failed miserably, and wrestled with a guilt-inspired drinking problem. As he describes it, "One night, I realized that hanging out in clubs and drinking all night long was going to kill me." He sold his drums for $800, and he and his wife got out of town.

Gary sort of stumbled into sales, connecting with Culligan Water Softeners, and, on the side, experimenting as an Amway distributor. Through those activities, he discovered goal-setting, self-improvement, and positive thinking, subjects he speaks about enthusiastically to his rapidly growing, nationwide organization of PWS distributors.

Discovering that they had a knack for MLM, Gary and his wife joined a fast-growing, new MLM, gave it their all, and in a very short time built a very large, profitable business—only to have the company go bankrupt. Gary determined that he would never again build a business that would always be at risk to someone else's management mistakes. He analyzed everything he'd learned from his MLM experiences, and designed his own marketing and compensation plan, for the new company, Personal Wealth Systems.

Gary's main twist was and is emphasis on marketing a collection of consumer services, discounts, and benefits all linked to a monthly magazine, as a subscription, not unlike an auto club or travel club membership, but more like a Price Club membership in that PWS's members have access to over 200,000 products. By focusing on the membership concept rather than individual products, a different kind of stability is possible: Customers/members and PWS distributors authorize the company to charge their credit cards or debit their checking accounts for a fixed amount of dues each and every month, unless they take action to drop out. This technique dramatically reduces turnover in the ranks, which is the bane of MLM.

He has also creatively combined direct-marketing media and methods with the multilevel business, so that PWS and its distributors (sales consultants) recruit additional subscribers and consultants with lead generation advertising, direct-mail campaigns, recorded messages, and audio and video brochures, rather than totally relying on face-to-face, person-to-person selling. This is the trend in the industry, and Gary is in sync with the trend most months, ahead of it now and again.

I've known Gary for a number of years, and watched with great interest as he has worked very hard to create a solid, stable business in a very fragile, volatile, highly regulated industry. What can be learned from Gary's example?

**MILLIONAIRE-MAKER STRATEGY #11:
CREATIVE COMBINING CAN CREATE HUGE
BUSINESS BREAKTHROUGHS.**

There's abundant evidence that you do not need something entirely new and revolutionary to make a fortune. In fact, having such a thing may be more of a liability than an asset! But there is great opportunity in combining the "old" in new ways.

Gary Haiser has combined the traditional, highly consumable MLM products, such as cleaning compounds, cosmetics, and nutrition, with the types of services customarily associated with union, association, or club memberships, such as a credit union and low-interest loans, health and dental insurance, long-distance telephone savings, and travel discounts, and put it all under one umbrella: the Personal Wealth Systems Savings Network. Then he has combined a very common, proven *direct*-marketing industry strategy, the continuity program, with the membership, as a means of reducing turnover and creating predictable incomes for his distributors. (Continuity programs, sometimes called "til-forbid programs," are used in direct marketing for book clubs, record clubs, movie clubs, recipe clubs, etc., where the customer enrolls for an automatic monthly shipment of goods and an automatic monthly charge.) Then he combined direct-marketing, mail-order, and even high-tech advertising methods with person-to-person selling. And he combined high-quality self-improvement, sales training, and even financial-planning training and services with his business opportunity to support the theme of his pitch to distributors: Use PWS as a vehicle to get out of debt and stay out of debt while still living well.

And all that's a lot of combining!

> **MILLIONAIRE-MAKER STRATEGY #18:**
> **CONSIDER PRIORITIES OTHER THAN THE**
> **FASTEST-POSSIBLE GROWTH.**

Some years ago, I watched several friends destroy their very young, explosively growing MLM company from the inside out. Their growth was so massive and uncontrolled that they couldn't fill orders, so products were constantly on back order; they couldn't get all the incoming data into the computers, so bonus checks were late; and they couldn't properly communicate with and enforce policies in the field, so overzealous and, in some cases, unscrupulous distributors were lying, cheating, and aborting the business's system at will.

This is only one of many times that I've seen growth turn negative. Gary Haiser's seen the same things, and has very deliberately insisted on conservative growth for PWS. Over the nine years that PWS has been in business, he has kept a grip on the reins of geographic expansion, product-line expansion and diversification, and corporate debt, and has stubbornly enforced policies, often at the expense of losing talented, productive people. My bet is that the long-term survival and stability of his company will prove his approach right.

When a business sacrifices product or service quality, financial controls, or integrity in favor of growth, it mortgages its future for immediate gratification—not unlike making a Faustian bargain.

MILLIONAIRE-MAKER STRATEGY #27: THINK BIG!

Gary Haiser certainly sees PWS as "another Amway" and more, as a multibillion-dollar business, not just a multimillion-dollar business. In fact, he'll tell anybody who'll listen that he's becoming "the Sam Walton of network marketing." You might be tempted to laugh at the idea of this funny little company beating Wal-Mart's $40 billion+ annual revenues. But don't laugh too loud. The ranks of the millionaire entrepreneurs are full of people who've been loudly and widely ridiculed for their big ideas, when they had nothing but big ideas. There seems to be a certain extra power or energy that comes from having very big goals.

Instead of Starting a Network-Marketing Company, Supply One!

Another way to reap profits generated by the unique duplication and multiplication of network marketing is as a supplier to one or more of these companies. In any given month, one-fourth to one-half of all new MCI residential customers come through Amway, so you can bet that MCI is very, very happy to be supplying Amway.

On a smaller scale, my client Eagle International Institute is a publisher of time-management courses, diaries, and systems. The Eagle Day Planner generates huge revenues as a supplier to several network-marketing companies. In its "regular life," Eagle competes head-on with products and companies like Day-Timers and Franklin, and conducts seminars for and supplies major corporations with time-management assistance for their employees. And that, itself, has grown into a phenomenally successful business. But in its "other life," Eagle private-labels and customizes its time-management materials and Day Planners for several different network-marketing companies, which, in turn, sell them to and through their proliferating distributor networks.

"The multiplication effect is staggering," Mark Colosi, the founder of Eagle International, told me, "because, in a multilevel company environment, everybody wants to be like the successful distributors they see and meet, and like their upline sponsors. So every distributor seen carrying around and using the Day Planner automatically influences other distributors to get and use the Planners. There's a snowball effect. The more who show up at a meeting with their Planners, the less comfortable those without Planners become. Soon, everybody's just got to have one.''

How Will the Market for Business Opportunities Stand Up in the Future?

If you have some kind of a business or moneymaking system you duplicate, or you supply someone who does, you can count on a continuing boom, with no end in sight. There are forces at work, many irreversible, literally flooding the market with people who must choose from self-employment options: buy a going business, start from scratch, buy a franchise, buy a distributorship, join a network marketing company, or enroll in a boot camp or similar training program.

Think about mid-level executives, for example. American corporations are in a downsizing mode, squeezing layers of middle management out, streamlining their bureaucracies, and, in the process, eliminating awesome numbers of jobs. So we have a fellow forty, forty-five, maybe fifty years of age, with twenty years or so into a management career, accustomed to earning $50,000 a year, probably considerably more, and his position is eliminated. And most companies that might provide him with a job are eliminating the same kinds of positions, too. He's too old to go back to school and too young to retire, but the jobs he may get offered will be inferior in status and offer considerably less income. He is firmly pointed toward self-employment.

Add the downsizing of the government in general, specifically the military, early retirements from government and private sectors, women reentering the workplace in droves, technical jobs replaced by evermore sophisticated automation, and you have a growing hunk of the population firmly directed toward self-employment.

There's also an explosion of interest in and start-ups of part-time, home-based businesses for another cluster of reasons. All these trends virtually guarantee that people marketing valid, duplicatable opportunities will do very well in the coming years.

Duplication of Another Kind, as a Private Labeler

Duplication can take many forms. By private-labeling his time-management systems for other companies, with their name and identity on them instead of his own company's, Mark Colosi takes an asset and duplicates it over and over again, with each one potentially as valuable as the original.

How an Oklahoma Beautician Became a Millionaire by Supplying the Multilevel and Direct-Marketing Industries with Her Home-Grown Aloe

At age seventy-four, my friend Edna Hennessee runs her sprawling cosmetics-manufacturing plant, aloe farm with sixty commercial-size greenhouses, and team of chemists, inventors, graphic artists, and account executives with an iron hand, a mother's love, and the energy of a teenager. Her multimillion-dollar enterprise has had much of its growth fueled by too many multilevel companies to remember, some gone, some still around, some growing explosively.

Edna's company is the only private label manufacturer offering home-grown, all-natural aloe from its own farms with complete formulation and packaging services all under one roof. The same fifty or so formulations that Edna created and produces are packaged for and sold by hundreds of different companies, including multilevel companies, TV infomercial companies, even the highest-priced, ritzy skin-care and beauty salons in New York and Beverly Hills.

And it all started in a pot on Edna's stove, in Lawton, Oklahoma. After six years of selling Merle Norman cosmetics and running a beauty salon, Edna decided she could produce better products than she was getting from her suppliers. Edna studied everything she could find at the library about chemistry and about cosmetics. In 1956 she formulated her first product, a face cleanser, in her kitchen, making eight or nine jars' worth at a time in a pan with a handheld blender. Two years later, her first line of products—"Youth in a Jar" lotions, creams, and treatments—was being sold in her own store, by mail, and by a few sales agents scattered around the country. Her business's explosive growth started when she switched from using water and oil as bases (common in the skin-care business) to using aloe as a base, not just a top-off ingredient. Consumers were thrilled with the effects of aloe-based products, and it wasn't long before other companies' executives were finding their way to Edna, eager to find out what she knew.

Edna kept her formulas to herself, and acted quickly to tie up as much aloe-plant production as she could. The only way to get this self-taught chemist's formulas, savvy advice, and top-quality aloe was to have her produce and package products for you. And hundreds of companies, including names you'd know, do just that.

> **MILLIONAIRE-MAKER STRATEGY #33:**
> **PRIVATE LABELING IS A FANTASTIC WAY**
> **TO GET MASSIVE DISTRIBUTION FAST,**
> **WITH NO ADVERTISING AND LITTLE**
> **MARKETING EXPENSE.**

Imagine what it must cost to create consumer awareness and demand for a new line of women's skin-care products! You'd need famous models and actresses, $25,000-to-$50,000-per-page ads in *Cosmopolitan* and other magazines, TV commercials, and fancy packaging. Could you invest a million before selling your first jar? That much and more.

For many entrepreneurs with great products or product ideas, creating consumer demand and building an entire business is beyond their reach. But if you control a great product, you can private-label it for companies that already have consumer confidence, advertising, and, most importantly, extensive distribution.

Let's assume you have an incredible new kind of car polish. You might package it one way for Wal-Mart, with their name, logo, and identity all over it, as "Sam's Favorite Polish." But you might also package it in a different size and shape container, labeled entirely differently for sale through The Sharper Image's catalog as "Sharper Image Auto Polish." And repackage it for a multilevel company.

Even a writer can use a version of private labeling, combined with recycling, to make money. Here's an example: Some years back, I thoroughly researched the subject of raising capital and borrowing money for business purposes from public, government, private, conventional, and unconventional sources, and I put together an audiocassette course on this subject (The Money System); my company has sold thousands of these cassettes, and continues to sell them today. I took that same course, altered its packaging slightly, and private-labeled it for Hume Publishing, for their use as a premium. I took chunks of that course and built a smaller audio product that was used by another direct marketer. Over about five years, I've recycled some or all of that same information into six different products, four of them private-labeled for other companies.

MILLIONAIRE-MAKER STRATEGY #34:
CREATE YOUR OWN TOLL BOOTH.

Edna set herself up in a toll position. There's a finite quantity of top-quality aloe vera in the country. Edna has the largest aloe farms in a ten-state area. But to get to that aloe, you have to go through Edna. Edna also created and kept confidential proprietary, exclusive, highly effective product formulations as well as expert know-how about how each item should be positioned, described, and demonstrated. To get that knowledge and expertise, you gotta go through Edna!

HOW TO MAKE YOUR MILLIONS IN THE EXCITING WORLD OF DIRECT MARKETING

There may be nothing more joyous than getting the day's mail, opening envelope after envelope after envelope and taking out—no, not bills!—orders with checks and money orders. And arriving at your office to find the tray of your fax machine filled with orders. And to walk through your office and hear your employees on the phone, taking orders. What used to be called "mail-order," the direct-marketing business today is almost irresistibly attractive. This is the world I live in the majority of the time. I have my own publishing/direct-marketing company, I'm a partner in another, and about half my consulting clients are in this business.

In this chapter, I cannot and will not even attempt to teach you direct marketing from A to Z, for two reasons. First, such a task is herculean; if you choose this as your main path to millions, you'll have to become a dedicated, determined student, read dozens of books, go to seminars, join several associations, and otherwise immerse yourself in self-education. The second reason is that there are aspects of the business I know little about and try to stay away from myself, such as the complexities of inventory and fulfillment management. Instead, I will zero in on only a few, hopefully eye-opening, opportunity-revealing ways that fast fortunes are made in direct marketing.

The One-Page Typewritten Letter That Brought in 7 Million Orders and Built an Empire

The company is now twenty years old; it sold to over 500,000 customers in 1993 and projects almost doubling that for 1994; it sells its products in thirteen countries—and it all began with a single, one-page typed letter that became one of the most-mailed sales letters in history.

In 1970 a young fellow struggling to succeed in mail-order after a series of abysmal failures was sitting in a dark house (the utilities went unpaid in favor of postage for sales letters). With an understandably unhappy wife looking over his shoulder, he decided to do the sales letter for his newest idea—a "family crest research report"—as if his life depended on it. The result was a very unprofessional-looking, typed, almost ugly letter, sent in a plain, typewriter-addressed envelope with a stamp on it, all to give the appearance of a personal letter from someone you know.

To date, an estimated 100 million copies of that letter have been mailed, all first class, pulling over 7½ million cash orders.

This letter made Gary Halbert both a millionaire and a living legend in the direct-marketing business. And, although he sold his interest in the enterprise early in the game, his letter built a continuing business that has become the world's largest marketer of family research publications and family crest–related merchandise: plaques, glassware, sweaters, shirts, and gift items. That company, Numa Limited, boasts a combined mailing list database of over 200 million people worldwide, organized not just by zip code (as all lists are), but uniquely by family surname. It's the only database of its kind.

Gary's original partner, Dennis Haslinger, has done a phenomenal job of expanding the company's products and services, creating strong customer loyalty, and applying very sophisticated marketing techniques to sustain this business. Can you hope to achieve that kind of success in direct marketing? Well, why not?

How Joe Sugarman Discovered a Powerful
Secret to Success in Direct Marketing

You probably know Joe Sugarman as the bearded guy on television selling Blu-Blockers sunglasses. But Blu-Blockers, built from a simple TV infomercial to a multimillion-dollar-a-year business, is only the most recent in a decades-long string of Joe's direct-marketing adventures and successes. In 1971 Joe Sugarman was the first person ever to attempt selling the then-very-new calculator by mail.

These days, we can buy an electronic calculator at Walgreens or Kmart for a few bucks. But maybe you remember when they were introduced, bigger, bulkier, and $200 or more. A product no one was sure the public would even buy. After all, did people really want portable calculators? Would they schlepp them around?

Joe fell in love with this device and believed he could sell it by direct mail. He raised $12,000 from a group of friends, ordered some calculators from the Craig Corporation, rented 5,000 names on ten different lists, wrote his sales letter, prepared an accompanying brochure, and launched his direct-mail enterprise. The first $240 order arriving in the mail was an exciting event. But the rest of the response was not so exciting. When the dust settled, Joe had lost half the capital. But then, getting ready to deliver the bad news to his investors, Joe Sugarman did something that has since become a cornerstone of his success philosophy: *He insisted on learning something from the apparent failure.*

One of the best benefits of direct-response advertising and direct mail is that you gain a considerable amount of information every time you advertise or mail. Your marketing is your market research and vice versa. It is relatively easy and inexpensive to test variables: one headline against another, one price against another, one media or list against another, and so on. In this business, if you have a little staying power and will listen carefully to your market, it will tell you how to succeed. It can be reasonably argued that the biggest secret to success in direct marketing is testing.

Joe went back and looked at the responses from each separate list. He discovered that eight of the ten lists had been horrible failures, but that two of the eight had worked well. If he had only used those two lists, instead of losing money, he would have made a 100 percent profit. In this case, the unsuccessful lists were, to Joe, the most logical, likely winners: engineers and accountants. The successful lists were made up of corporate presidents and high-level executives.

"When the list broker urged me to test those lists, I thought corporate presidents did not have the time to read long sales letters and advertising literature. And that the mail would be screened by their secretaries. And that they wouldn't want a calculator anyway. Certainly an engineer was a better prospect. But," Joe admits, "I was wrong."

Joe now "owned" a very valuable "asset": He knew what type of people would buy calculators by mail.

Armed with this discovery, and eager to move quickly before calculators became commonplace and cheaper as he believed they would, Joe marshaled more capital from his investors and a new partner, who owned a mailing service, secured lists of only the newly defined ideal prospects, and mailed 400,000 pieces, risking a staggering $100,000. "There were a few anxious days, as the response started to trickle in," Joe remembers, "but then it started to *gush* in. More than we could have imagined. Our home was no longer our home, it was a factory processing calculator orders. We were selling more calculators every day than Sears was nationwide."

Joe subsequently made a specialty out of marketing new and unusual electronic gadgets, using direct-mail and copy-intensive full-page ads in the *Wall Street Journal* and the airline magazines. In his JS&A ads he introduced the first liquid crystal digital watch, a pocket-sized CB radio—his biggest success, selling 250,000 units at $39.95—and the first mass-marketed, easily installed home security system in 1977, and employed the very first nationwide toll-free 800 number for placing orders in 1973.

For several years, you couldn't open an airline magazine without seeing one or more of the JS&A ads packed with copy.

Unfortunately, Joe lost his entire business in an expensive, much-publicized battle with the Federal Trade Commission. (His company failed to ship on a timely basis, thanks to an enormous snowstorm that shut down his plant and wiped out his computer system.) But, he started over with a new direct-marketing business out of his garage, and began creating winning promotions all over again. His fascination with new sunglasses that blocked out certain types of ultraviolet rays led to Blu-Blockers, a product that has made Joe a multimillionaire for a second time. Even if you wanted to chalk up the JS&A success story to luck, Joe's achievements since then have proved that he employs success principles that are timeless and reliable.

I should add that Joe never finished college, never took a course in advertising or creative writing, and, generally speaking, had no qualifications for his phenomenal success. This happens to be another very appealing aspect of direct marketing: It is an industry filled with unqualified successes. You can learn it on the run. I never went to college, never took a course in advertising, and entered the direct marketing field with zero qualifications. My client, Greg Renker, now head of a $200 million direct-marketing corporation, was doing marketing for a hotel and resort, and brought no special qualifications with him to direct marketing. Gary Halbert was a door-to-door encyclopedia salesman. You can succeed here, too.

> **MILLIONAIRE-MAKER STRATEGY #39:**
> **PROPERLY VALUE INFORMATION,**
> **ESPECIALLY WHEN GAINED THROUGH FAILURE.**

Failure has a bad rap. While many people are terrorized and paralyzed by it, most direct-marketing pros live with it as part and parcel of their daily existence; just about everybody in this field has more losers than winners to their credit. I can show you, for example, eight full-page direct-response ads I developed in the course of 1992 and 1993; six are dead-bang, irredeemable losers, two are home-run, million-dollar winners. So I failed six times out of eight, or nearly 80 percent of the time.

The winners more than make up for the losers economically, but of at least equal importance is that each of the six losers has immense value to me. I learned from each one. And the information gained from each failure, more often than not, has value to future applications far in excess of its cost. You have to view your unsuccessful products, ads, sales letters, and promotions as investments, not losses, and then take the time and exert the energy to extract useful information, so that you get a good return on your investment.

If Joe Sugarman's $100,000 Gamble Turns Your Stomach Sour, There's a Less Risky Way to Get into Direct Marketing

When I was working on an infomercial about the direct-marketing business, featuring Joe Cossman (see chapter 3), I met and interviewed many people who had started different direct-marketing businesses and mail-order enterprises, many of them novices, like Carol Nieman. Carol secured the mail-order rights to a product called "The Calypso Beverage Holder," made by a foreign manufacturer—a little doohickey that sticks to a car's dashboard, has a floating disk inside, and keeps your cup level regardless of the bumpiness of the road or the quick turns you make while driving. Instead of marketing her product direct to consumers at her expense and risk, Carol solicited established catalog companies to get them to sell the product for her. She succeeded in placing the product in just one catalog, and her profits for the first three months exceeded $10,400.

Carol took no *risk, paid for* no *advertising, didn't even fill orders, but she made $10,000 in the direct-marketing business!* Her story illustrates one of the most tried-and-true, least risky paths to profits in this business: providing a winning product to established catalog companies.

Last year, there were more than 12 billion catalogs mailed in the United States alone. Over 110 million Americans made a purchase by mail or phone from a catalog. There are over 10,000 companies doing all or some of their marketing by publishing and mailing catalogs. That group includes everything from 500 top, well-known catalogs, such as The Sharper Image, Spiegel, Lillian Vernon, Herringtons, and Hammacher Schlemmer, to thousands of smaller, specialized catalogs serving niche markets, such as Bass Pros Shops catalogs or Smith & Hawken gardening products catalogs. There is a catalog for just about every business, hobby, recreational activity, or interest. *And the two things all these catalog companies have in common could make you rich.*

How the Catalog Industry Could Make Your Million for You

First, most catalog companies make the majority of their profits from repeat sales to a core group of loyal, exceptionally responsive customers. This is a very important fact for you to understand. It creates the need you can fill that could make you rich.

Because of this fact, the second thing every catalog company has in common is a need to keep coming up with new, interesting, and different products to rotate in and out of their catalogs to keep their customers interested and buying. That means the catalog industry's doors are wide open to you as long as you meet relatively simple criteria. In fact, their buyers are eagerly waiting for you to show up!

When you place your product with catalog companies, their established, successful direct-marketing machine goes to work for you: Their smart, experienced advertising people rework your sales copy; their photographers and graphic artists work on a presentation for your product; their capital advertises your product in tens or hundreds of thousands of catalogs; you get endorsed access to their lists of responsive buyers; and their telephone order-takers work for you. In some cases, vendors and suppliers are required to put up some money against costs, especially if they're trying out an untested and unproven product. But in many cases, the catalog company simply buys products from you at a discount, resells them, and bears all the risk and expense of doing the selling. That discount will range from 50 percent to as high as 70 percent. That may sound like a lot until you consider that when you market directly to consumers via space ads, direct-mail, television, or other means, your costs of sale may very well exceed 50 percent and go as high as 70 percent.

I have had my books, cassette courses, and other products sold for me in a number of top business product catalogs, including Day-Timers, Caddylak Systems, Nightingale-Conant, Sybervision, and the Miles Kimball Business Book, as well as lesser-known, specialty catalogs, like National Response Corporation's Insider Report. Although this has been a very small part of my business, I'd guess that, over the years, I've sold at least $500,000 worth of my products this way, maybe more. Many of my clients extract huge incomes from the catalog industry's sale of their products. The Guthy-Renker Corporation, for example, had over $5 million worth of its products, like PerfectSmile, sold through catalogs last year.

So, how do you get your products into catalogs? Obviously, you need to be the prime source (the manufacturer, publisher, or importer) or have exclusive rights and be able to afford the economics of this type of marketing. You also need to do your homework and select the most likely catalogs for your particular product. Then you need to prepare a convincing presentation: sales copy, examples of ads that have worked, proof that the product will sell, articles that have appeared about the product, and anything else that might help command the attention of a catalog buyer. You can approach catalog companies directly, in person, by mail, by phone follow-up, and by exhibiting at trade shows, or you can use the services of any of a number of manufacturers' agents or brokers specializing in representing products to catalogers.

There are other, related opportunities, too. One of the most interesting cataloglike situations is having your product sold through other companies' credit card statement mailings. There are over 60 million credit card holders that can be reached this way. Companies that accept this type of advertising include Texaco, Mobil, and most other oil companies, American Express, Diners Club, Discover, most MasterCard and VISA programs, and a number of national department and clothing store companies. Tests are usually done in 50,000 "chunks." Often, just like with catalogs, you can get your product purchased from you at wholesale and advertised and resold by this method at no risk or cost to you.

Recently, for example, a StairClimber fitness device has been sold with inserts in Marathon Oil credit card statements; Michele Easter's video about saving money on groceries is sold by Amoco; how-to-dance videos are sold by Amoco; the Microcrisp product seen in TV infomercials is advertised in Montgomery Ward statement stuffers; and the ThighMaster has been sold in many companies' statement mailings. The directories and contacts you need to get your products sold by catalogs, stores, and other established distribution channels are listed in chapter 13.

**MILLIONAIRE-MAKER STRATEGY #28:
GET OTHERS TO DO YOUR SELLING FOR YOU.**

There's no law that says you have to risk or invest your own money in order to make money. When you own or control a promotable product and have publicity for that product, success with that product in one medium, and other proof that it is a salable product, you have assets just as valuable as money. Others whose main assets are in the distribution category—customer databases and relationships, catalogs, and other media—need you and your products as much as or more than you need them.

If You Want to Advertise Your Product Direct to the Public, Here's a Secret That Kills a Lot of Novice Direct Marketers

Take a look at these circulation figures and just imagine what could happen if you had a hit with an ad for your product in one of these magazines:

Modern Maturity . . . . .22 million+
TV Guide . . . . .15 million+
Better Homes & Gardens . . . . .8 million+
Popular Science .2 million

. . . even these specialty magazines:

Vegetarian Times .200,000+
Motorhome . . . . .140,000+

. . . or how about *USA Today?*

Heck, if just one-tenth of 1 percent of those readers order, I'll be rich, rich, rich!

That particular dream has destroyed more fledgling mail-order entrepreneurs than I can count in this lifetime. Here's why: How you buy your space and what you pay for your space is at least as important as your product, offer, and ad, maybe even more important. The dirty little secret here is that the successful, repetitive, direct-response advertisers are not paying anywhere near list price or retail ("rate card") for their advertising space. If you do, you'll go broke.

If you naively call the typical magazine and try to negotiate your own advertising placements, you'll usually be quoted their rate card prices, less discounts ranging from 15 percent for acting as your own agency, 2 percent for cash, maybe another 10 percent if you commit to multiple insertions or a flat "mail-order advertiser discount" roughly equivalent to a combination of all of those. Either way, you may think you've done pretty well. But you're not even close to where you need to be.

Direct-response advertisers need to get space at 50 percent to 70 percent off rate card in order to make money. Many publications never make those kind of discounts available directly to individual advertisers. Instead, there are quantity buyers who negotiate exclusive arrangements with these publications, buy all their remnant and standby space and guarantee the publication a certain amount of revenue, and, in return, obtain discounts as high as 80 percent off rate card. These bulk-buying groups are, frankly, the closely guarded secret of direct-marketing professionals like myself. We help our clients work with these bulk buyers.

However, you can negotiate your own huge discounts with many nonmajor publications, such as trade magazines, special-interest magazines, weekly or community newspapers, and association publications. For example, I have one friend (who has asked not to be named) with a successful full-page magazine ad who targets thirty magazines, sends the ad to all of them along with a check for 20 percent of their rate card price for a full page, with a letter that basically says:

> Keep this ad and check and if you have unsold space in any of your next three issues, run my ad and cash the check. If you do not have space available on this basis within the next three months or you do not wish to hold this ad on a standby basis, please return the uncashed check in the enclosed, preaddressed envelope.

In a typical month he'll get five or six takers out of the thirty. A few more will call him, counteroffer, and negotiate.

Negotiating media gets easier as you go along, too. If you have an ad repeatedly appearing in a magazine, other competitive magazines' representatives or, with small publications, the owners will seek you out. In such situations, you can often negotiate a very good "test rate" on your own. We have magazines, card decks, and other media agreeing to test rates 50 percent to 60 percent off their rate cards, even occasionally on a pay-per-inquiry or per-order basis, after they've seen our ads appearing repeatedly in competitive media.

> **MILLIONAIRE-MAKER STRATEGY #40:**
> **SELLING BRILLIANTLY WON'T MAKE YOU**
> **A MILLION IF YOU'RE NOT BUYING SMART!**

There's no telling how many people have stepped up and tried ads in one media or another, lost money, and given up on their ideas when, in truth, their ideas, products, and advertisements were good enough to generate profits and build a business if they weren't grossly overpaying for their advertising!

One of the top negotiating experts in the country, Chester Karrass, uses this line in his ads: "In life, you don't get what you deserve—you get what you negotiate." Unfortunately, the media business is not unlike the car business, with a multiplicity of prices, discount schedules, and confusing terminology all concealing the bottom-line, rock-bottom, minimum "real" price. As a direct-response advertiser, though, you have an enormous advantage in negotiating ad costs: Unlike most of a media's traditional advertisers, you actually know how well your ad works in each place. You have precise results. You know what your cost of advertising per sale is in Media A vs. Media B. And the media people know you know. So you can use this data to say: "This is all we can afford to pay for space in your magazine, in order to get the same cost per sale we get with these other two magazines."

The Basic Decisions You Need to Make
If Building a Business
Through Direct-Response Advertising

There are several basic, foundational decisions to make if you're going to sell products and build a business through direct-response advertising. First, will you use one-step or multistep advertising? One-step advertising is the simplest method; Joe Sugarman used it with JS&A. The ad directly sells the product and, hopefully, makes a profit on that first, direct sale. In multistep advertising, an ad is placed that usually offers something for free, such as a book, report, brochure, video, or catalog; it's usually called a "lead generation advertisement." Then the sale and profit are made by one or more follow-up mailings, plus, possibly, outbound telemarketing. This is the approach used by NordicTrack, one of the largest direct-response advertisers today. Each approach has its own pros and cons, and you should carefully investigate the appropriateness of each to your particular product, media, and market. Generally speaking, you'll have more success with lead generation advertising and multistep follow-up than one-step advertising, although one-step is obviously simpler and, thus, an easier business system to operate.

A hybrid approach I've had considerable good fortune with is what I call "self-liquidating" or "zero-cost lead generation." With this method, a very-low-cost item is offered for sale in the initial advertising, which is intended only to screen out the lowest-quality leads that are always collected with free offers and to cover most or all of the ad costs.

Let me give you a great example of self-liquidating lead generation. One company I own an interest in sells a relatively expensive home-study course ($600), but it never advertises that product. Instead, all the advertising is for a low-priced introductory book ($19), which includes both useful information and lengthy sales presentation for the product. The book costs about $2 to print and deliver; the $17 "profit" serves only to offset all the advertising costs. The company's real profit is made on the sale of the course.

Next, you must decide whether you will be front-end or back-end oriented—and that has nothing to do with anatomy! It is increasingly difficult to make your money on the front end, the *first* sale to the customer. Most people who do make millions in direct marketing do so by building long-term relationships with customers who buy a number of products from them over time. The profits come from what I call TCV, Total Customer Value. If you are going to build a business rather than try getting rich from one-shot sales, you have to give thought to how you will develop and expand your product line and how you will continually communicate with your customers. In other words, you need to strategize beyond the first product and the first sale.

A Classic Example of a Business Built
Through Direct-Response Advertising

I believe that Gerardo Joffee is one of the smartest mail-order entrepreneurs ever to openly and generously share his methods in a book, *How You Too Can Make at Least One Million Dollars in the Mail-Order Business*, and I urge everybody to buy it. The first business Joffee built was Haverhills, which was a household name in the 1970s. Haverhills did most of its marketing through its own catalogs of kitchen, household, travel, and electronic gadgets and unusual products, handpicked by Joffee, and described in clever, interesting copy. Joffee obtained the bulk of his customers using the self-liquidating approach to advertising I described above. The main product he used was a multipurpose knife he named MACK THE KNIFE, offered for just $1 in magazines such as *The New Yorker*. His most frequently used ad was a tall, thin, one-column ad, with a full-size picture of the knife standing up, and this copy run alongside:

SUPERSTITIOUS?

In our most compulsive desire to make new friends, we had decided to GIVE AWAY a whole truckload of MACK THE KNIFE . . . a masterpiece of Vulcan's art. At home, in kitchen, glove compartment or on a camping trip self-appointed experts have nominated versatile MACK 'Knife Of The Year.' But alas, our generous impulse was thwarted by one of our superstitious supernumeraries who officiously insisted that giving away a knife is very bad luck and in order not to kill an incipient friendship (and to ward off the evil eye) we should assess a token charge. Reluctantly

giving in we agreed to charge $1 for MACK (although he lists for $4.95 in our catalog) AND— that isn't all. For that same $1 we'll also send you our Color-Full Catalog and a $2 Gift Certificate (good for your first purchase). If you think this is an unusual offer, you're right. Better take advantage of it before our accountant returns from vacation and reads us the Riot Act.

In the large quantities he purchased, Joffee got these knives for thirty-five cents each, and all the costs of handling and ful-fillment added another twenty-five cents, giving them a forty-cent-per-unit contribution to ad cost. At the time, it was routine for that contribution to pay back almost all or all of the costs of the advertising, providing them with thousands of new customers from each ad with zero acquisition cost. This strategy attracted enough customers to build Haverhills in just five years from a standing start into a company that Joffee sold to Time, Inc., for $1 million (see chapter 11). Of course, the days of the one-dollar self-liquidator are dead and gone. We are working with costs increased over twenty years since Joffee's successes. But the strategy still works in an endless number of applications.

**MILLIONAIRE-MAKER STRATEGY #29:
ACQUIRE CUSTOMERS FOR FREE ANY TIME,
ANY WAY, EVERY TIME,
AND EVERY WAY THAT YOU CAN.**

If you are doing your job right, each customer has a certain value beyond the initial sale, so you can afford to invest up to the profit of the first sale in order to acquire the customer. I have one client who acquires about one-fourth of his customers with a $99 sale. His costs are $55 in advertising and direct-mail follow-up to make the sale, $35 for the product, $3 for credit card processing, and $1 contribution to overhead, for a total of $94. He is only keeping a measly $5. But he'd cheerfully give even that up if he had to, because he knows that nearly 50 per-cent of those customers will turn around and buy $400 to $800 worth of merchandise, at full markup and profit, from him within six months. With that as a known fact, his number-one job is pouring as many new $99 customers into his funnel as he possibly can, from any and every source he can find, even if he does so by giving away the entire $99.

Is Having Your Own Catalog the Ultimate Goal of a Direct-Marketing Business?

Probably. Most companies begin with the entrepreneur somehow advertising and promoting just one or two products, then, as the customers accumulate, he expands the product line, offers them other, related products, and soon decides to assemble all of his products into a catalog.

Richard Thalheimer started The Sharper Image selling only jogger's wristwatches and stopwatches. Lillian Vernon started out advertising monogrammed handbags and totebags in magazines. Ted Nicholas started Enterprise Publishing with his book *How to Form Your Own Corporation Without a Lawyer*. And I could continue this list.

The lure of having and mailing a catalog is the economy of scale, compared to mailings on behalf of single products and offers, and the streamlined simplicity of the business. I put out my own catalog each year for exactly these reasons. However, I want to warn you that they are "lazy" reasons. With his permission, I'm going to quote Gary Halbert, who tells about his experiences with his first catalogs.

Many years ago, after Dennis Haslinger and I got our family coat-of-arms business cranked up, we decided to produce a catalog. It seemed like a good idea. It appeared to be a natural. You see, our front end product was an 8½ × 11" piece of parchmentlike paper upon which was printed a line drawing of the earliest family crest ever recorded with a particular family name. This "family name research report" also had a brief history of how that name came into being. Now, naturally, a lot of people who bought this inexpensive little report were fascinated, intrigued, and pleased enough to want to see their family coat-of-arms in full, authentic, heraldic colors in a variety of products, such as wall plaques, china plates and cups, drinking glasses, napkins, stationery, and so forth.

So off I went into the woods of southern Ohio. All by myself. To camp out and create a catalog. I worked and worked and it really turned out neat. It featured cute pictures of my three small sons, billed as product testers, and approximately seventy items, most of which could be customized with your family crest. The catalog measured 5½ × 11" and was printed on glossy stock in full color.

After it was finished, I had a bunch of them printed up and mailed out and I sat back to wait for the results. They sucked. We didn't even break even. I said to myself, I wonder what would happen if I eliminated all the loser products and then mailed a smaller catalog or simple brochure? I did analysis [and] found that only three of those seventy products were carrying all the weight. Everything else was dead meat. Those three products, by the way, were all wall plaques. So I designed a simple color brochure that featured only those plaques.

What happened? Actually, it wasn't very exciting. All we did, after mailing those brochures to our customer list, was break even. But I was moving in the right direction, wasn't I? So then I took the top-selling wall plaque, had a color photo taken of it, and I sent a replica of that photo along with a personal style sales letter to our customers.

And we dragged in millions of dollars.

What all this can teach us about what most catalog mailers do wrong is [that] they mail too many catalogs and not enough simple letters! When I told Ed Mayer [the "dean" of direct mail] about my catalog experience, he said that if everybody who now mails catalogs would instead build an individual direct-mail promotion around their top items, they'd make a lot more profit.

That doesn't mean I think everybody who mails a catalog should stop. Not at all. What I do think, however, is that *most catalog mailers should look at their catalogs as information-gathering devices.*

Let's say we've got a big catalog mailer who is going to push out 3 million catalogs next year. In my opinion, this mailer should send, instead, only about 300,000 catalogs. Next, he should analyze his response and then create a sales letter and simple brochure describing each of the top sellers from the catalog. Then these should be mailed as individual direct-mail promotions at about three-week intervals.

Even though I do not do that in my own business out of laziness and a willingness to knowingly trade off a certain amount of profits for convenience, my own experience tells me that Gary is right. And, although the company he left behind uses catalogs, and has made these catalogs perform profitably, it also relies on a solo-mailings strategy similar to what Gary just described.

This means that the catalog is neither the panacea nor the ultimate goal. Instead, it should be viewed as one weapon in a multiweapon arsenal, to be used for certain purposes at certain times, but not relied on entirely if maximum profit is your objective.

However, If Anybody Says You Can't Start a New Mail-Order/Catalog Business from the Kitchen Table and Succeed Anymore, Tell 'Em That's "for the Birds"

In 1990, in the midst of the recession, Peter Deutsch and Carol Curtis started Creative Bird Accessories, a catalog company serving pet bird enthusiasts. She was a school nurse, and he owned a furniture business tied up in Chapter 11 bankruptcy. But their research had revealed that there were 52 million pet birds in the United States, 175,000 subscribers to *Bird Talk* magazine alone, and pet bird owners' associations and conventions.

Peter also invented a shoulder perch that featured a big pouch to catch bird droppings. In the fall of 1990 they advertised the perch for the first time in *Bird Talk*. The perches sold faster than he could make them.

In 1991 Carol quit her job to work on getting out their first catalog: a six-page "mini" mailed to 5,000 names, most of them purchasers of the perch. Soon the catalog grew to twenty pages, the mailing list to nearly 20,000. In 1994 they hit sales of $200,000 a year, still operating out of their home, with very restrictive resources. Direct marketing still offers plenty of opportunity for gutsy entrepreneurs to start new businesses from scratch and quickly experience substantial success.

Here Are the Exact Ingredients for a Direct-Mail Moneymaking System of Your Own

Ingredient #1: The Lists

First, you need a list of prospective customers for your product or offer. In a hierarchy of quality, the very best list is that of present and past customers who know you, have purchased from you, and have been satisfied, to whom you are now making a new offer; next best are people who have taken the initiative to demonstrate current interest in what you have to offer by responding to your advertising; next best are commercially available, rented lists of purchasers of related products; bringing up the rear are rented lists of compiled prospects, such as people of a certain age, occupation, or financial demographic.

Even people like me, who make a living writing copy and creating direct-marketing materials, will admit that at least half the success or failure of a campaign depends on the quality of the list—not on our brilliance. I'll even go further and tell you that a poorly written sales letter can get good results if it is matched to just the right list. But the greatest sales letter ever written could fail if mailed to a very poorly qualified list.

Incidentally, most businesses underutilize their own customer lists. As a consultant, I frequently get to be a hero simply by getting my clients to mail more offers more frequently to their past and present customers.

Ingredient #2: The Offer

In direct marketing, the offer usually includes an appealing product or products (or service/services), a discount, a premium or bonus, a strong guarantee, and an added reason to respond promptly. This is all spelled out as "you get this . . . and this . . . and this." To state the obvious: The more attractive the offer is, the better.

Ingredient #3: The Mailing

Mailings can range from simple postcards and flyers to complex, costly catalogs. More often than not, I rely on a sales letter to present my offer. And beginners to direct-mail selling will do well to master the use of the letter before using more complicated or expensive materials.

I've written an entire book that reveals and demonstrates my twenty-eight-step system for creating an effective sales letter— *The Ultimate Sales Letter*—and I believe that just about anybody can follow that system and do well. Without referring to that book, though, let me tell you a few of the most important things you need to know about sales letters.

Long letters tremendously outperform brief letters, contrary to what most people assume. I often use letters eight to thirty-two pages in length. Your letter should be as long as is necessary to thoroughly, persuasively tell your story, not written to fit a certain predetermined length. The only way a long letter loses is if it's boring. For that reason, your letter should replicate you, your personality, your enthusiasm for your product, much the way you would personally, conversationally tell a friend about it. And there are some simple, reliable formulas taken from person-to-person selling that work well in sales letters, such as

AIDA: *A*ttention, *I*nterest, *D*esire, (call to) *A*ction. Or: State the Problem, Emotionalize the Problem, Solve the Problem.

If you're a rank beginner in creating sales letters, you can start your education by studying the sales letters you get. There are a number of good books about selling as well as about sales letters at your library and local bookstores. And you can hire professional copywriters to do your first projects for you, while you learn.

Along with the letter, you may have enclosures. There may be a flyer or brochure, a page of user testimonials, a reprint of a favorable article about the product, and an order form. Whether the order form is separate or incorporated in the letter, it is very important. Your order form needs to clearly tell the customer what you want him to do and how he is to respond. It should also summarize the offer.

Can You Dial Your Way to a Million Dollars?

Sophisticated direct marketers are increasingly combining outbound telemarketing follow-up with direct mail to dramatically increase overall response and actually improve the relationship with the customer. Although a mailing program itself may produce a response of 1 to 3 percent to as high as 7 to 10 percent if directed at established customers, it is not unusual for a combination mail–telephone call campaign to increase a response of 2 percent to 15 or 18 percent, and a response of 7 to 10 percent with established customers to 30 to 35 percent.

I often work with and recommend InfoCision, one of the top outbound-telemarketing firms in the country specializing in the "relationship call." This means two things: First, they will not do cold outbound telemarketing for any client. There must be some relationship already established—at the very least, the person being called must have responded to some type of ad and requested information. Second, they will not use high-pressure tactics or otherwise endanger the relationship between the person being called and the company they are placing calls for. This is an extremely intelligent approach.

How Smart Outbound Telemarketing
Made a Fast $2½ Million
for a Fitness Device Manufacturer

Maybe you've seen the Easy Glider commercials, infomercial, or other advertising. Easy Glider is an inexpensively made aerobic ski machine, selling most of the time for just $59.95. The same manufacturer makes a much more elaborate, sturdier, enhanced version of the same product, called Fit One, that sells for $400. The manufacturer realized that their 600,000 Easy Glider purchasers, because they were fitness buyers, would be prime candidates for Fit One.

With the assistance of the people at InfoCision, a strategy was developed to mail literature to the Easy Glider buyers that extolled all the virtues of Fit One, and then call them and offer them the full $59.95 they paid for the Easy Glider as a trade-in discount toward the Fit One. In a very short period of time, this strategy generated about $2.5 million in Fit One sales that would probably not have been realized any other way.

How a Carefully Constructed Telemarketing
Plan Put Sports Sciences in the
Swing of Things

Here's another example of telemarketing intelligently applied, courtesy of Steve Pittendrigh and Lisa Mueller at Info-Cision: Sports Sciences manufactures and markets The Pro-Swing System, a computerized golf swing analyzer that uses a light beam and sensors to generate corrective feedback. It's sort of a Dr. Spock approach to golf. This doohickey sells for a fat $300, and runs off a software program called AccessLinks. A list of AccessLink software owners was obtained and a package of literature about Pro-Swing was mailed to them. InfoCision timed telemarketing calls to closely follow arrival of the mail.

And they employed one of their "secret" strategies: using tele-marketers with a genuine interest in the product being offered. In this case, they used only those employees who played golf and were familiar with computers for this project team. These telemarketers could talk the same language as the customers.

Because most AccessLink owners had purchased the software as much for its fun uses as for skill improvement, the tele-marketers' basic script emphasized Pro-Swing's uses as an innovative, entertaining, and supersophisticated computer game, not just its original purpose as a tool for correcting the golfer's swing.

Employing this carefully constructed, telemarketing-driven marketing plan, Sports Sciences converted over 5 percent of the AccessLink owners to their customers, yielding over $500,000. This also gave Sports Sciences an instant database of its own customers, which they could communicate with by mail, phone, or both, to offer additional products and services.

New Frontiers in Electronic Direct Marketing

Some of today's most interesting and exciting direct-marketing opportunities are in TV home shopping, TV infomercials, radio infomercials, and other "information superhighway" frontiers. All of these are discussed in the next chapter.

> **MILLIONAIRE-MAKER STRATEGY #1:**
> **DIVERSIFY IN MARKETING, TO FULLY EXPLOIT**
> **TOTAL CUSTOMER VALUE.**

In the 1990s, largely thanks to the alarmingly high costs of acquiring new customers, few direct marketers can lazily rely on just one or two methods of selling to and communicating with their established customers and their prospective customers. Instead, a diversified approach is necessary, carefully choosing from a cafeteria of methods, testing them, and ultimately assembling them in just the right order for a particular line of products, company, and clientele.

SUPERHIGHWAY TO MILLIONS: THE BRAVE NEW WORLD OF ELECTRONIC DIRECT MARKETING

I'm in a hotel room in Chicago, after having presented a three-hour evening seminar. I doze off and wake up at 1:15 A.M., and channel surf with the remote to see what's on television. On five of the eleven channels available on my TV set, there are infomercials. Three of the five are "mine"—one I produced for a client, and two are owned by a consulting client. I'm getting royalties on two of the three. For the last fifteen minutes, I've been making money while sleeping.

The Incredible Power of Television

Somehow, in the wee hours of the mornings, enough bleary-eyed folks set aside their remote controls, pick up the phone, and call in and order Victoria Principal's skin-care products, *Entrepreneur* magazine's *Be Your Own Boss System*, which I coauthored, Vanna's tooth whitener, The Big Green Clean Machine, exercise doohickeys, car wax, diet foods, self-improvement courses, spray paint for bald heads, and Oriental woks—enough to make millionaires of a surprisingly large and growing number of entrepreneurs.

My longtime client the Guthy-Renker Corporation is an interesting case study for three reasons: (1) its business is driven by TV infomercials; (2) it has a sophisticated development of businesses within businesses, like those little Russian dolls nested one inside the other; and (3) its management philosophies make them interesting.

In 1978 Bill Guthy started an audiocassette product–manufacturing company, which initially focused on recording conventions and conferences, and products for professional speakers. He started out of his apartment, with a combination of new and used, bought, borrowed, and begged equipment; a vague belief that there would be major growth in spoken-word audio products; and a goal of developing the largest company of its kind in the audio industry. Today, Cassette Productions Unlimited (CPU) has both a West Coast and an East Coast plant with state-of-the-art technology; it is the largest company of its kind, and the major audio product manufacturer for the entire infomercial industry. CPU also owns Audio Renaissance, an audio publisher of books on tape, poised for growth tied to the current expansion of books-on-tape departments in bookstores and books-on-tape stores.

By Paying Close Attention to How His Customers Were Selling Their Products, Bill Guthy Spotted a New Opportunity

In the early 1980s, as CPU produced millions of cassettes for the earliest infomercials, Bill became interested in the high-margin retail end of that pipeline instead of the low-margin manufacturing end. A cassette he might make twenty cents on by manufacturing it for a customer might be sold by that customer for $9 to $15, against his cost of less than $1.

In 1986 Bill acquired the audio rights to Napoleon Hill's classic *Think and Grow Rich* and his other works. Along the way, he met Greg Renker, who was then marketing director for the Indian Wells, California, Racquet Club, and discovered that Greg shared his fascination with infomercials and his commitment to Napoleon Hill's *Think and Grow Rich!* philosophies, and had good marketing instincts, useful contacts, and capital to bring to the table. Together, they produced the first "Think and Grow Rich" infomercial and aired it frequently in 1987, as well as an improved, second version in 1988. Both were financial hits, bringing in over $10 million, which at that time was a big number for the infomercial business.

Neither Bill nor Greg had the slightest experience with TV show production or TV advertising, but they had a number of other successful infomercials to study and from which to extract principles of success, as well as their own ideas about improving the appeal and credibility of the infomercial. From the very beginning, they elevated the image and sophistication of infomercials. "Think and Grow Rich" was the first to use a significant celebrity as a host (Fran Tarkenton) and the first to use well-known, credible individuals as testimonials, such as Tom Monaghan, head of Domino's Pizza; Mary Kay Ash of Mary Kay Cosmetics; Wally "Famous" Amos; and Senator Jennings Randolph.

Like most things I do, I got involved in the infomercial business by dumb, happy accident. I met Bill and Greg when I sold a company to Cassette Productions Unlimited. Bill then invited me to find a way to rework "Think and Grow Rich II" to bring its sales performance up, which I did, and I have been consulting with them ever since. (In the case of "Think and Grow Rich," I restructured the offer, added premiums costing about $2, and raised the selling price by $50. We went on to sell tens of thousands of units. I'd guess my tinkering plunked an extra $500,000 in Guthy-Renker's coffers just from the premium cost-to-price increase differential. They were hooked on me, and I was hooked on television.) Guthy-Renker skyrocketed from a $10 million company to a $100 million company in just a few years, and is doubling again as I put this book to bed.

To show you the several different ways you might make millions through TV infomercials, I'm going to give you the background and current state of the union of the industry, reveal more of the Guthy-Renker secrets for success, and take you inside my extensive work in this industry.

How the Problem of Falling Seminar Attendance and Ronald Reagan Accidentally Combined to Launch the Infomercial Business

In 1984 President Reagan's penchant for deregulation prompted the Federal Communications Commission to drop its limits on the length of commercials, giving networks, broadcast stations, and cable stations freedom to sell time in virtually any size blocks they chose. In that same year, Ray Lindstrom, a Phoenix-based promoter of "get rich in real estate" seminars featuring a guru named Paul Simon, was watching seminar attendance decline while the costs of filling the seminars rose, and was looking everywhere for a solution.

A Million Dollars Made in Two Days

On a whim, Ray brought a video crew in and taped one of the seminars, bought a number of one-hour blocks on two cable networks, and literally threw it on the air to see if people would watch at home and then call an 800 number to order Simon's cassette course on real estate investing. By today's standards, the infomercial was downright primitive: The speaker at the front of the room gave his regular talk, using hand-drawn slides on an overhead projector before a small audience in a poorly lit hotel room. The first weekend this ugly little production aired, from less than $80,000 in media, they sold nearly $1 million worth of courses.

In 1985 Ray and a partner, Nancy Langston, bought nearly 3,000 hours of cable TV time for a total of about $8 million dollars, and produced over $21 million in sales of the Simon courses. In its coverage of this phenomenon, *The Hollywood Reporter* snidely noted that "the population of real estate millionaires didn't noticeably increase, but Lindstrom and Langston became the leading marketers of home study courses. Their success quickly brought imitators." In fact, imitators proliferated like rabbits.

**From a Get-Rich-Quick Business Largely
Populated by Snake Oil Salesmen and
Assorted Oddballs to a Very Sophisticated Media
That's Almost Certainly Here to Stay**

In its early years, the infomercial industry was populated by get-rich-quick promoters knocking off Paul Simon and promoters of very questionable (and often FDA-attacked) health devices and potions and cheesy gadgets, mostly hawked by their inventors and authors, no-name hosts and hostesses, or an occasional long-in-the-tooth celebrity, and it all worked almost in spite of itself. Media was incredibly cheap; the stations and networks were slow in recognizing the enormous profits being made by these "weird" advertisers, and happy to be paid for time in the dead of night rather than paying for programming, usually reruns of ten-year-old TV shows nobody wanted to watch anyway. Insomniac audiences were fascinated and, according to some industry critics, fooled by these new kind of shows. Mostly thanks to the cheap media, many people put infomercials on the air, made millions of dollars almost overnight from the initial sale alone, and treated the entire business like an electronic version of the gypsy's wagon with the snake oil pitchperson.

Three major forces contributed to substantial, relatively rapid change. Beginning about 1989, academic critics, regulatory agencies like the FDA and the FTC, and some congressmen began holding the infomercial up to scrutiny, and didn't like what they saw. Second, a few sizable companies led by people with the vision to see past the fast buck, notably Guthy-Renker, were succeeding with higher-quality shows offering higher-quality, honestly advertised, and honestly guaranteed products. Third, the first big jumps in cost of media time started.

In 1990 Greg Renker led a group of infomercial CEOs and producers in forming and funding The National Infomercial Marketing Association (NIMA) to both self-regulate the industry and to lobby Washington and the media on the infomercial industry's behalf. NIMA has been effective in both jobs.

Today's Infomercial Business: An Enormous Area of Opportunity, If You're Careful

Today, the average infomercial costs no less than $80,000 to $250,000 or more to produce and another $15,000 to $30,000 to test. Then it is ready to "roll out" and air frequently on a mix of national cable, superstations, and area broadcast stations for months or even years. I have worked on a number of infomercials that have generated over $50 million each during their lifetimes. However, both risk and media cost are skyrocketing, and media availability is increasingly competitive. Overall, only one in sixteen infomercials make money; fifteen die in testing and are buried in Tax-Loss Cemetery only a few days to a week after completion. The viewing and buying public is harsh in its rejection of these "losers."

Of course, certain product/topic categories work better than others. For example, weight loss, skin care and beauty, kitchen gadgets, and moneymaking opportunities have been proven very reliable. Products that are preventive in nature, such as crime prevention, or those that feature long-term, distant benefits, such as information about paying off your mortgage faster or investing for retirement, have been tried many times and failed miserably more often than not. Beyond product selection, those of us who do a lot of work creating products, offers, and infomercials have our own lists of factors that try to predict a show's probability of success. Given the right combination of factors, with experts creating the show and smart media buyers, the risk falls from 16 to 1 to about 4 to 1.

More importantly, the way money is made from infomercials has changed. Instead of getting rich quickly from the initial sale, many infomercials often air at break-even or slightly better than break-even as a means of acquiring huge numbers of customers rapidly, without acquisition cost, so that profits can be made via repeat and subsequent sales, direct mail, outbound telemarketing, and other means. The infomercial has shifted from a get-rich mechanism to a very attractive means of building a business that you intend to stay in for the long haul.

Guthy-Renker mirrors this trend perfectly. After ''Think and Grow Rich'' Guthy-Renker had a megasuccess with the first of a series of ''Personal Power'' infomercials showcasing motivational speaker Tony Robbins, with hosts like Fran Tarkenton and actor Martin Sheen. The database of the Personal Power customers became a business in and of itself: Other Tony Robbins titles, a continuity or subscription program to ''Power Talk,'' a monthly cassette series, seminars, and more are sold to these customers. This taught Guthy-Renker a model for developing a vertical business within their company that is the game plan behind over half of the infomercials they produce today.

Their Principal Secret skin-care infomercials with actress Victoria Principal have provided the biggest and most promising of such businesses. Through these infomercials and Victoria's related appearances on the home shopping channel QVC, over $75 million in skin-care products have been sold. But the bigger, much more profitable business is in perpetuating a relationship with those customers. Only six products are sold on television; there are over forty products in the entire line, with new ones constantly in development. There is a Beauty Club, automatic bimonthly shipments of products and product kits, seasonal promotions, and a catalog.

It's important to understand that most mail-order/catalog companies have to lose money on acquiring new customers through advertising; in essence, they are ''buying'' their customers, so the ability of the infomercial to rapidly plug 100,000, 200,000, or even 500,000 new customers into a direct-marketing business at zero acquisition cost is very appealing. That's why Fingerhut, the largest direct-mail marketer of consumer products in America, jumped into the infomercial business in a big way in 1992.

MILLIONAIRE-MAKER STRATEGY #32: DEVELOP VERTICAL BUSINESSES WITHIN YOUR BUSINESS.

Guthy-Renker has built their vertical businesses linked to different celebrity spokespersons and personalities, so that there is a Tony Robbins business, a Victoria Principal business, a Vanna White business, etc., and this is extremely powerful because consumers relate and bond better with individuals than with corporate entities. But vertical businesses can be built under product brand names, business names, or other identities.

How You Can Get in the Game—and Win!

First, you may have a product or collection of products and other assets to bring forward that a major infomercial company will want so badly, and be unable to easily duplicate, that they'll take you on much like a publishing company takes on an author: They'll pay you an advance against royalties (sometimes) and a royalty on all sales; they'll pay all the costs of producing, testing, and airing a show; and they'll either develop a negotiated joint venture with you on the "back-end" business, the continuing, long-term relationship built with the infomercial-generated customers, or manage that business in its entirety, too, and pay you another royalty.

The benefits of this can be tremendous. Being adopted by such a parent brings expert analysis, strategic planning, script-writing and creative talent, ample capital, usually a major celebrity host, already-in-place 800-number order-taking, credit card processing, fulfillment, accounting, management, legal counsel, media buyers and media time, and even noninfomercial product distribution—such as to catalogs, other mail-order venues, home shopping channels, and retail stores—all together without a dime's worth of risk on your part. When Guthy-Renker takes on a project, for example, there are typically two to three product development specialists, one of several top producers and his team, an additional scriptwriter, and one or two direct-marketing consultants all put to work on its behalf.

There are negatives. First, just like an author who signs on with a publisher, you usually give up all control over the project as well as certain exclusive rights to your product. Second, you'll probably receive royalties in a range of 2 to 6 percent of gross; on $1 million of sales, you might make no more than $50,000.

Third, in most cases, you'll now share the control and income from everything else that can be done with the customer acquired through the infomercial.

These no-money-out-of-pocket deals are increasingly difficult to get done. Five years ago, infomercial companies were begging for products. Now the deal flow going to them is simply amazing. And some of the things and people they turn down are equally amazing. However, if you have a truly hot product or other idea that seems to lend itself to an infomercial, and you own or exclusively control it, you may want to try and place it with a big infomercial entity on a royalty basis. In 1995 so far, I've negotiated two such deals for clients, and have three more pending. It can be done.

The second big opportunity is to fund, produce, own, and control your own infomercial and the business it can build. There are a number of reasons to go the independent route. If you want to generate leads rather than directly selling a product on the infomercial, if you've been rejected by the big guys but believe they're wrong (and they often are), or if the idea of making three to four times as much profit is extremely attractive, you may want to go independent.

And, yes, there's still plenty of room in the marketplace for the independent. One of my clients, U.S. Gold (see chapter 6), has been airing its independently produced show for five years straight and building its business. Another independent I assisted made over $60 million in two and a half years. Another infomercial I scripted and helped develop for a major was dropped by that company, bought by the inventor of the product sold in it, aired independently, and has since done tens of millions of dollars in sales and launched extensive mail-order and retail distribution of the product. By my best estimates, that show made its owner a millionaire in six months.

Roughly half of all my work in the industry is with independents. As of this writing, I'm handling one project for a large international travel conglomerate, another for a start-up entrepreneur who has pieced together his capital and, in the grand tradition of our free enterprise system, is "rolling the dice." *In this business, they each have about the same chances of success.*

It's a pretty level playing field. However, it's extremely important to remember that the lion's share of opportunity and profit is in the back-end business. I am constantly counseling clients to do an infomercial only if they have a strategy, a product line, and an ability to build a continuing business on their customers.

A third, huge area of opportunity is in getting involved as a vendor to the infomercial industry. This industry is a billion-dollar consumer of video production and other creative services, printing, publishing, packaging, audio and video duplication, private label manufacturing of every imaginable product, in-bound and out-bound telemarketing services, premiums, computers and software, and on and on. And because so much happens so fast, a vendor who is exceptionally service-oriented, can meet tough deadlines, and is reliable can capture substantial chunks of business in this industry.

A fourth area of opportunity is in joint ventures, piggyback arrangements, parasite arrangements, and distribution. Every successful "As Seen on TV" product works exceptionally well in mail-order catalogs, in inserts in credit card statements and newsletters, even in stores. And every successful "As Seen on TV" generates a database of customers that will be mailed to frequently, for which additional products are needed.

In *parasite marketing* you, the product marketer, capitalize on ("feed on") some other successful company's customer database and resources. This is often done with an *endorsed mailing*: The owner of the list sends out a complete direct-mail package to his customers that includes a letter of endorsement of your product. *Piggyback marketing* is also parasitical, but a costly separate mailing is not done. Instead, literature for your product may be added to (piggybacked) with the host company's monthly statements, other mailings, or packages.

The financial terms of these deals vary and are negotiable. In a pure parasite marketing situation, you put up no money. The host company not only provides the database but also pays all the marketing costs. Joint ventures are more common. In a typical joint venture, the host company might provide the database and the labor to physically do the mailing, while you would pay the costs of preparing and printing the materials for the mailing.

Maybe you have a customer list, newsletter, mail-order business, store, or other type of distribution that should be selling some successful "As Seen on TV" products. Or maybe you have a product that won't work as a lead item in an infomercial, but can be sold to all the customers created by a particular infomercial.

Incidentally, it's important not to prejudge the infomercial customer. While most people might guess it's folks of very modest means—*National Enquirer* readers and Kmart shoppers—the statistics tell a very different story. Half of the buyers of the Personal Power products, for example, come from the top 20 percent income segment of the population. And industry surveys show that infomercial buyers are aware of the sales content of the shows, enjoy them, feel better informed by them than by other types of advertising, and, of those who buy from them, the majority are satisfied and predisposed to buy from another infomercial.

MILLIONAIRE-MAKER STRATEGY #9: BEING ALERT!

Bill Guthy learned of the opportunity that would make him a multimillionaire by being very alert to what was going on in his customers' businesses. I'm always amazed when I talk with a manufacturer, printer, or other vendor who can't describe their customers' businesses. "That company that buys 25,000 books a month from you," I asked a printer, "what do they do?"

"I don't know," he said. "They're in something having to do with mail order." Well, if I were that printer, able to buy paper at truckload wholesale prices and print stuff for myself in off-hours and slack times at bare-bones cost, and I was supplying somebody moving 25,000 books a month, I'd have my curious nose stuck right into their business. Wouldn't you? I hope so.

Right now, I own half of a business running full-page ads in a handful of magazines every month, doing very well, that may put as much as an extra $100,000 in my bank account this year with almost no effort, all because I paid very close attention to what a copywriting client of mine was doing, discovered a new area of opportunity, and found a way to get in the game without conflict of interest.

It is incredibly important to have your opportunity antennae up at all times!

MILLIONAIRE-MAKER STRATEGY #12: "PLUS-ING."

When they produced the "Think and Grow Rich" infomercial, Greg and Bill took what was working repetitively in the infomercial business at the time and found a way to use that as a foundation, but also to take it up a notch and go it one better. People who were closely associated with Walt Disney are the first people I heard using the term *Plus-ing* to describe this, and they tell me that Walt emphasized this over and over again: How can we take a "known," something that works, and then make it or do it a notch or two better? He taught that plus-ing defied mathematics—it produced multiplied results. And that's actually what he did with Disneyland; he took something that already worked and was popular, an amusement park with rides and snack vendors, and plus-ed it.

MILLIONAIRE-MAKER STRATEGY #44:
DISCOVERING AND USING "FORMULAS."

The objective of every savvy marketer and entrepreneur ought to be to find a reliable formula for success that can be repeated over and over again.

When Greg and Bill plus-ed the infomercial, they did it with three main ingredients: a recognizable, respected celebrity host; testimonials from famous people as well as happy customers and users of the product; and improved production values, comparable to "real" television. From the success of "Think and Grow Rich," they were astute enough to recognize that this was a formula for success with value beyond the one application. As a result, you can see that very same formula applied in the "Personal Power" infomercials and in other Guthy-Renker successes.

How an Independent Won: Perfect Swing Builds the Perfect Business with Its Own Infomercial

In 1989 Peter Herrold bought the small company making The Perfect Swing Trainer after practicing with the product took twenty strokes off his golf game. The product is a big, bulky circle within a circle, constructed of PVC pipe, on a sturdy stand, with adjustable rings. It "forces" the person into a perfect swing over and over again, so that "muscle memory" is created in the "golf-specific muscle." Find that hard to believe? So did an awful lot of golfers, so the company struggled until taking a big gamble on television in 1992.

Peter had reached the conclusion that the product had to be demonstrated and dramatized before people would believe in it enough to plunk down $400 or $500, so he decided to switch his entire advertising budget from magazines and the ad campaign that was keeping the company in a survival mode into the vast unknown of the infomercial world. To keep costs to a bare minimum, the company relied on its own understanding of how to sell the Trainer, hired local videotape crews, and produced its own infomercial. Peter also hired his own in-house telemarketers to handle the optimistically anticipated responses from the infomercial.

His gamble paid off. The response to the infomercial was immediate and dramatic, more than doubling sales from the previous year, and providing over 100,000 customers predisposed to buy other Perfect Swing products. As I'm completing this book, the company is completing production of its new, much-improved infomercial and just may double sales all over again, thanks to the power of television.

If You Think Infomercials Are Amazing, Wait Until You Hear the Story of the Home Shopping Channels!

Just about everybody knows what a Tupperware party is. Picture it: a dozen women gathered in a living room for the express purpose of watching various kitchen gadgets and storage containers demonstrated so that they can find something to buy. Now imagine that same Tupperware party with a captive audience of 10 million women in the living room, and you have an idea of what a home shopping channel is all about.

Unlike the infomercial viewer, sitting there with remote control in hand, ready to click out the second she's bored, the home shopping channel viewer has set aside her remote control, placed the phone in her lap, has her credit card at the ready, and is waiting for something to be offered that she can buy. Selling to an audience like that is a unique situation.

Getting your product sold on a channel like QVC or HSN can make you a millionaire in a matter of days, weeks, or months. These companies have a large amount of their available time committed to already proven products being periodically, repeatedly presented. They also get many products that flip over from successful infomercials. These companies reject 90 percent of all products presented to them, and choose from thousands of new submissions every week, so breaking through is difficult. Most new products are placed with QVC or HSN through a small number of professional brokers and brokerage organizations, like my own or those listed in chapter 13. But there are other ways to break through. For example, early in 1995 QVC conducted a highly promoted, open, new-product search tour to a dozen U.S. cities, and it was so successful they're almost certain to do it again. Many people got their products sold on QVC by going to those advertised events. If you exhibit at trade shows, the home shopping channels send buyers to virtually every merchandise show held. You can even assemble a package of information about your product and submit it directly, unagented, over the transom to these companies, although I don't recommend this approach.

You enhance your chances of successfully getting your product sold on QVC, HSN, or one of the less-known shopping channels if your product is highly demonstratable or visual—after all, we are using television here! It should also solve a problem or match a need or desire that is universal, because home shopping channels are mass marketers, who sell to the general public. Celebrity spokespersons or endorsers are helpful but not essential. Proven success in other direct-response environments, such as print ads, catalogs, direct-mail, or TV commercials is also helpful but not essential.

How a Visionary Entrepreneur Built an Entire Business Around a Celebrity: The Story Behind Joan Rivers Products

One of the best examples of a home shopping channel–created millionaire is my client Mark Kress, founder and president of Joan Rivers Products. You've probably seen Joan Rivers on the home shopping channel QVC, presenting her jewelry or hosting her TV show *Can We Shop*. And you probably thought little about it. But behind those scenes, there's a fascinating business success story.

In 1989 a young man by the name of Mark Kress was fired from his position as vice president of entertainment marketing at a major broadcast network. His firing occurred just one week before he was to receive a six-figure commission for new business he had secured. At that moment, he made the decision never to work for anyone else again. "If something was going to get my attention sixteen hours a day and keep me up nights worrying, I was determined to profit from it in a big way," Mark says. "Hey, nobody says your vision has to be poetic!"

So, fueled by the new determination to succeed as an entrepreneur and accustomed to earning an excellent income that had to be replaced, Mark stepped up to the plate in a big, bold way. He made some guesses about the future, and took some pretty big risks based on those guesses. Mark saw the future of marketing in his television. Specifically, he saw home shopping via television as the growth industry of the nineties—and, in retrospect, that was a pretty good guess.

Mark also knew from his experience in the entertainment business that the difference between mediocre and extraordinary success for a new product or a new business was often a celebrity endorsement. *Finally, he conceived of a new strategy that would have four parts:* the right celebrity, that celebrity's full involvement and commitment to the business, the right products, and marketing via television.

This Business Was Built Backward!

Mark then did something very unusual. Instead of first creating or assembling products, getting a business going, choosing marketing methods, and, finally, maybe adding a celebrity spokesperson, he chose to get the celebrity first, then create a business to fit. Compared to the way most businesses evolve, this was a backward approach.

With this unusual plan in mind, Mark faced his next obstacles: He didn't know any celebrities, he did not want to go through the usual bureaucratic dealings with Hollywood agents, managers, and lawyers, and he didn't want the usual insincere, for-the-money-only endorsement arrangement. He also didn't have enough capital to launch a business even if he had the right celebrity in his pocket. Many might call that combination of obstacles insurmountable, but, if there is one theme I'm trying very hard to demonstrate in this book, it is that no combination of obstacles is insurmountable. If your idea really has merit, and you have sufficient determination, you can get past the most incredible obstacles.

Anyway, Mark racked his brain, rummaged through his correspondence files, talked to his friends, and, finally, he thought of a contact—a Beverly Hills cosmetic surgeon who had intimate relationships with a number of celebrities and their altered anatomical parts. Mark knew the doctor only slightly, through a charity they were both involved with. "I was willing to knock on the door of this possible opportunity," Mark recalls, "even though it was a long shot. Many people stop short of exhausting every possible opportunity. I didn't. So I called this doctor, convinced him to meet with me, went and told my story, and got him excited about my plan." The doctor arranged meetings for Mark with celebrities and the doctor became an investor, providing much-needed financial backing. Of the celebrities Mark met with, Joan Rivers was the one that stood out as right. And Joan bought into the new idea of building an entire marketing business around a celebrity.

Joan Rivers is known for comedy, and for bouncing back from very difficult career and tragic personal life circumstances, but she is also known for style. She frequently makes media "Best Dressed" lists, and has an almost obsessive interest in fashion. Mark's research revealed that jewelry was a top-selling product category in the home shopping medium. All of that came together in the decision to provide home shopping viewers with classic, quality jewelry at affordable prices with Joan as the line's on-camera, sincerely enthusiastic spokesperson.

It's important to note that, exactly as Mark intended, Joan has been much more than just a celebrity spokesperson. I'm fortunate to have Joan Rivers Products, Inc., as one of my clients, and I have seen firsthand how thoroughly involved Joan is with product selection, jewelry design, and decisions in every aspect of the business. The huge success of this enterprise has a great deal to do with their working together this way, so she can *honestly* talk about *her* products.

Joan Rivers Products began in the spare bedroom of Mark's house in Los Angeles. Mark and his wife had to learn the jewelry business from the ground up. And they had to risk: Joan invested only her persona and her time. So Mark and his wife tapped their savings and mortgaged their home to provide their share of the capital. They personally guaranteed credit lines. And, in September 1990, Joan Rivers went on the air, on QVC, for the very first time, with thirty jewelry designs to present. No one had any idea what would happen.

In the first three-hour airing, 27,000 orders representing over

$1 million were taken. "That was small by our standards today," Mark says, "but more than enough reason to break out the champagne that night. QVC had never successfully sold costume jewelry before. There can be only a few things in life sweeter than the moment when a nerve-shattering risk like this one pays off in such a big way."

Mark and Joan have since sold as much as $6 million worth of jewelry in one eight-hour period and, in total, well over $100 million worth of jewelry. New products, new catalogs, and a new series of self-improvement seminars, books, cassettes, and an infomercial are all on the horizon. I've been privileged to work with Joan and Mark on the development of these "You Deserve to Be Happy!" seminars and self-help materials. ("You Deserve to Be Happy!" is based on Joan's own experiences in recovering from grief and adversity, creating career, business, and personal breakthroughs, and achieving happiness and peace of mind.)

As I worked with Joan on this new product, it was interesting to see that many of the principles for happiness and success that she believes in and uses parallel those Mark has used to create this business in the first place. For example, Joan tells people to "break the rules" in order to achieve great things—Mark broke a whole book full of rules about how you start a new business.

**MILLIONAIRE-MAKER STRATEGY #36:
YOU *MUST* FIND WAYS TO USE THE POWER
OF TELEVISION. IT IS *THE* MOST
POWERFUL FORCE IN AMERICAN SOCIETY.**

It is arguable that no other media have greater influence, impact, and power than television. A single appearance on a talk show puts an author's book on the bestseller list. A politician's career is made or destroyed. You cannot ignore the growing power of television, so isn't it incumbent on you to find a way to use it to your advantage?

Now, What About the Really High-Tech Opportunities? Information Superhighway or Super Hype-Way?

Publishers and marketers are in a mad scramble to find ways to profit from the much-publicized explosion of the so-called information superhighway. A considerable amount of advertising and direct marketing is being attempted, with varying levels of success, via the on-line services, CompuServe, Prodigy, and America OnLine. Of even greater interest to the entrepreneurs I deal with most is the vast network of independent computer bulletin boards and the enormous linked network of people on the Internet. One consultant described this to me as an opportunity to do the equivalent of printing and mailing and delivering a million sales letters at the push of a button at no cost.

Quite frankly, it ain't that simple.

For example, readers who use computer bulletin boards will immediately be familiar with what these folks call "flaming." When someone inappropriately delivers unwanted advertising, everybody blasts them back with negative messages, and broadcasts their displeasure to other users of that bulletin board or service. This is sort of like having a few thousand people you've sent sales letters out to all show up on your doorstep as an angry mob.

I confess that I am computer-inept. I grudgingly use one as a word processor, and travel with a laptop I use in the same way. But I do not have a phone modem, I don't use any of the on-line services, my eyes glaze over at computerspeak, and I have to force myself to learn about new opportunities where the computer stands between me and access. The truth is that I dislike computers so much that if we had a gun at home we'd be getting new computers at least once a week.

Fortunately, I have a consulting colleague who is my opposite in this regard, and who has been making a very detailed study of all this for some time. Ken McCarthy spent several years designing sophisticated on-line information systems for

Wall Street traders, so he understands the technology. Ken is also a savvy, successful direct marketer, so I trust his opinions. I asked him to provide a brief contribution to this book about what we are calling "on-line marketing," and here it is:

> With all the hype surrounding this entire area of opportunity, getting straight answers isn't easy, and most of the practically accessible marketing opportunities are only visible on the horizon, not yet here. But you'll need time to prepare yourself to take advantage of them, so I'll make some suggestions about that.
>
> Everything that is currently available in hard form—print, audio, video, and interactive disk—will be available on demand through the personal computer. For example, a prospect will be able to dial in and see your demonstration video with the same ease they now call an 800 number to hear your recorded message. That's where we're headed.
>
> There will be instant on-line delivery of advertising, much of it on request, of actual purchased information, and extensive on-line ordering. I would emphasize that those who are going to profit the most from these new opportunities are going to be the people who've mastered good, old-fashioned selling skills and can translate them into any media.
>
> To prepare and stay in step, there are five things you can do right now:
>
> 1. If you don't already have one, get a personal computer and a modem.
> 2. Join one or more of the major computer on-line services—Prodigy, CompuServe, or America OnLine —and begin to familiarize yourself with the on-line environment.
> 3. Learn how to use E-mail, and start including your E-mail address in your ads and business communications. If you're like most people, after a little

experience with E-mail, you'll prefer it over the phone, the fax, and "snail mail" for routine messages.

4. Subscribe to *Boardwatch Magazine* and seriously consider attending one BBSCON, the annual gathering of computer bulletin board operators. You can learn more about the reality of the information highway and make more useful contacts by attending this one conference than from a year of reading and study.

5. Above all else, start making friends with the technology and the people who understand it. It's not necessary to become a computer expert to profit from new technology any more than it is necessary to know how to make your own ink to be a successful copywriter, but you do have to have reliable people you can work with and who will steer you in the right direction.

What's the payoff for all this effort?

Every time a new media has emerged, the marketers who figured out how to make it work first enjoyed tremendous, once-in-a-lifetime, windfall profits. It happened with radio. With broadcast television. With cable, infomercials, and TV home shopping. It will happen with computer bulletin boards, too.

It's already beginning in a few niche markets.

Take Paolo Pignatelli, for example. He's the proprietor of The Corner Store, a company based in Connecticut that specializes in selling software. In 1993 he had sales of over $1 million without spending a nickel on advertising. His method of promotion is simple: He makes himself available to answer software questions on CompuServe. He ran his last traditional print ad in 1992 and has never looked back.

HOW A FLORIST HAS SALES BLOOMING AT OVER $100,000 A WEEK!—ON-LINE

Bill Tobin and Peter MacMurray of PC Flowers have shown how a basic, everyday business can be transformed by clever on-line marketing. Using Prodigy as a base, their "order it online" florist service became the tenth largest retailer in the 25,000 FTD system in its first five months in business. They now do well over $100,000 worth of business per week, and have started a second business, PC Balloons.

One of the ways they keep in touch with their customers, by the way, is with a newsletter that offers flower-care tips and arrangement suggestions. It's delivered every month electronically—no printing or postage costs!

These pioneer-examples will suggest obvious opportunities and applications to many people who read this chapter. And, by the very nature of a rapidly emerging technological environment, we'll all be behind by the time this is published. Entrepreneurs, small business owners, and big companies will all find many ways to profit in these ways. It is here, and it is coming, that's not open to question. The only question is how soon you'll be involved.

Three of the Best High-Tech Marketing Tools That I Do Understand!

Okay, so I'm behind the times with computers. Ken and some of my other friends are dragging me, kicking and screaming, onto this superhighway thing, so don't worry about me. In the meantime, there are three readily available, semi-high-tech marketing tools that I *do* understand that you should know about:

1. The simple but incredibly powerful "free recorded message." *Here's a marketing insider's secret:* The offer of a free recorded message in an ad or sales letter, either as the means of response or an optional means of response, can *increase response by as much as 500 percent.* The theory I have to explain this has to do with nonthreatening first contact. Many people interested in your proposition may still be reluctant to

pick up the phone and call, knowing the person on the other end is going to "sell 'em." But if that person knows he's calling and getting more information from a recorded message, he's safe. The free recorded message also allows you, in some cases, to run smaller ads—you wait to deliver much of your message in the recording, only to those interested enough to call and get it, rather than paying money to deliver it to everybody.

There are other advantages, too. Such a message lets you deliver your message in a warm, friendly, reassuring voice, with enthusiasm and inflection. If you like, the message can be recorded in more than one voice, include testimonials, and even utilize sound effects. If you use a celebrity in your marketing, the message could be done in the celebrity's voice. The listener can't skim; he either listens or he doesn't. Most services handling these calls for you can track and tell you how many calls you get, how many hang-ups at one minute, at one and a half minutes, at two minutes, etc., so you can make adjustments to the length and content of your message. The services will take calls to hear your message twenty-four hours a day, seven days a week, and they have multiple-line capability, so callers do not get busy signals. Most can do name and address data capture for you. And it's all relatively inexpensive.

At the conclusion of such a message, you can refer the listener back to calling your regular office number, or you can use voice prompts to let him leave his name, address, phone, even credit card numbers to order or request literature electronically, or you can give the caller the option of instantly switching from the recording to a live person by pushing a button.

2. Fax-on-demand. Let's say you have twenty different products, each requiring a four-page sales letter. You can create twenty fax-on-demand numbered "boxes," and put those twenty sales letters on file in them. Then anybody with a fax machine can call your number, enter the code number for the product that interests them, enter their fax number, and instantly receive the sales letter that explains that particular product.

Many companies with complex, sophisticated products are using this as a means of making a variety of technical support information available to their customers, conveniently, on demand. But I believe there will be more and more marketers finding ways to use fax-on-demand.

3. Broadcast fax. With broadcast fax, you can instantly have the same fax sent and simultaneously delivered to 10 or 10,000 different fax machines anywhere in the country. However, my limited experience warns against using broadcast fax on an unsolicited basis. Junk fax is such an annoyance to recipients that they often fight back by faxing you 100 blank pages, for example, or complaining to regulatory agencies. But if people give you their permission, then broadcast fax is fast and efficient, and has the impact of delivering by Federal Express but costs pennies instead of dollars. For example, a group of VIP subscribers to my newsletter have furnished their fax numbers and asked to receive special bulletins and offers by fax. If I'm putting on a seminar, I can fax the invitational brochure to those people.

Last year, one of my clients had a new product to introduce to their customers, and they needed some fast cash flow with nominal investment. We devised this strategy: A cheap one-page sales letter was sent to all the customers, briefly describing the benefits of the new product, and offering them advance notice and a discount offer by fax, but they had to call and ask for it. The response to the mailing was about 3 percent; the order rate from those then faxed an eight-page sales letter was 90 percent!

I experiment with and use technology, but am careful to avoid being seduced by it. The smartest marketers and entrepreneurs will devote a carefully determined amount of time, energy, and money to learning about and testing each new technology-driven media and opportunity as it comes along.

9

HOW TO PRINT AS MUCH MONEY AS YOU WANT, LEGALLY: THE INCREDIBLE WEALTH-PRODUCING SECRET OF INFORMATION PRODUCTS

There is one type of product that is the perfect product for direct marketing and for mail-order. Fortunately, it is a product anybody can learn to create, inexpensively develop, manufacture, control, and exploit.

I Print My Own Money Every Day

As you hopefully know, making your own money on the copy machine in your office or the printing press at your buddy's quick-print shop is illegal. The U.S. government is pretty firm on the idea that they should be the only ones allowed to print up more money any time they need some.

You can, however, do the next best thing, legally: Turn ordinary paper into information products people will pay for. What is an information product? It can be a book, like this one, or a manual in a three-ring notebook, or a spiral-bound book, or a simple report, copied on a photocopier and stapled in the corner. Or audiocassettes, videocassettes, software disks, or any combination thereof. It can even be a recorded message people pay to hear, with no hard material involved in its manufacture at all.

All you need to be in this business is information people will pay for and access to something as simple as a photocopier. These days, personal computers with desktop publishing capabilities have made the preparation of printed information products easier than ever, but there's still a lot of money being made with simple products prepared on an ordinary typewriter.

This is the business I work in the most with my own companies and with clients. In this chapter, I'll tell you more about the types of information products that make fortunes, the marketing of information products, and introduce you to some remarkable successes.

The diversity of successful information products is amazing. Many of these products have to do with hobbies and recreational interests. Several years ago, Patti Carlson sold millions of dollars' worth of her How to Play Piano Overnight kit via direct-response television. Today, Robert Laughlin sells a home-study course, How to Play Your Favorite Songs on the Piano in Just 3 Hours—Without Reading Music or Taking Piano Lessons. *100 Delicious Hawaiian Recipes You Can Easily Make at Home* is a simple booklet advertised and sold through classified ads in tabloids and women's magazines.

Many information products are business- and occupation-oriented. Joe Sabah has sold thousands of his 104-page booklet *How to Get the Job You Want and Get Employers to Call You* by being a guest on radio talk shows (see chapter 10). There are three different entrepreneurs I know who successfully sell booklets, plans, and kits on the topic Making Money at Home as a PVC Furniture Manufacturer. The least expensive booklet sells for $10; the most expensive kit for $150. Hume Publishing Company built a huge business selling its Successful Investing course as a subscription, using direct mail. Many information products focus on health and fitness, privacy protection, travel, beauty and fashion, and games and gambling.

As you can see, the only thing these products have in common is that they are information. They deal with very different topics and interests, they have different price points, they are comprised of different media, and they are advertised and sold through different methods. And I could just as easily list 100 more.

The Incredible Financial Leverage Secret of Publishing on Demand

I first started to print my own money in earnest in 1978. Shortly after I became a professional speaker and joined the National Speakers Association, I discovered that, with my background in advertising, marketing, and sales, I knew more about how to get bookings and clients than many people who had been involved in the speaking business for years. I created an ugly, cheap, homemade four-page catalog of Special Reports on different topics appealing to my speaking colleagues, with titles like:

> How to Find Hidden Markets for Your Speaking Services
> What to Write in a Simple Letter to Get Meeting Planners Eagerly Calling You (Never Make a Cold Call Again)
> How to (At Least) Double Your Fee Every Time You Speak With After-the-Fact, Follow-up Product Sales
> 17 Most Common Mistakes Made by Speakers with Their Brochures and Demo Tapes—and How to Avoid Them

I can't even find this old catalog or any of these reports now, but as I recall there were about twenty different titles priced from $3 to $15 each. Each one was four to no more than twenty typewritten pages. And I used what we now call publishing on demand; I never printed up any inventory. I had the typewritten originals in plastic page protectors and, when an order came in for a particular report, I took those originals off the shelf, stuck them in the photocopier at the Kwik-Kopy down the street, made the one report or reports that I needed to fill that day's orders,

put them in envelopes and sent them out. Now this little project,
with my simple, dirt-cheap catalogs sent out to only about 2,000
speakers, brought in over $11,000 in about a month. Some or-
dered one report, most ordered two, three, or four, a few ordered
ten or even all of them. A report I sold for $3 cost about 40
cents to photocopy and 20 cents to mail. A big chunk of that
$11,000 was profit.

I learned three valuable lessons from that simple, primitive
experience very early in my career: (1) The value of targeting a
particular specialized market and creating information products
of great interest exclusively to those people; (2) that what you
can charge for information products has virtually no relationship
to what they cost to make, only to the value of the content to
the buyer, which means you can build incredibly high markups
into these products; and (3) that you could make them as needed,
avoiding tying up even a penny in inventory, so all your available financial resources could go into marketing (where, in my
opinion, they belong).

Now, I have a confession: today, eighteen years later, my
(part-time) million-dollar-a-year collection of information products publishing businesses isn't a whole lot more sophisticated
or complicated than my first primitive reports project. In one of
my businesses, I have twenty different information products,
ranging from a simple spiral-bound manual (that sells for $69)
to kits including six to twelve audiocassettes, videotapes, 200 to
300 pages of written instructions and examples in a three-ring
notebook, divided into sections, and separate reports (the kits
sell for $399). In another business, I publish a monthly business
newsletter, a monthly travel newsletter in another. And, in a third
business, I develop information products for sale by other publishers. Of all of these products, only a few are manufactured in
substantial quantities in advance of their sales and warehoused.
Most are published on demand.

Consider one of the kits on a very specific topic. Depending
on what I'm doing and how I'm advertising, in any given month
we may sell 20 or 30 copies of this particular product; in other
months we may only sell two or three. I have no interest in tying
up money in putting 500 of these things on the shelf. So, here's

what happens: This week, orders for three copies of this product come in. The masters of the audiocassettes are taken off the shelf and, in a tabletop high-speed duplicator, three copies are made, then labeled. The originals for all the written materials are put through the photocopier and three copies are made. Universal notebooks with clear plastic sleeves on the cover, which we can use for many of my products, are taken out of inventory and this product's cover is slipped into the sleeve. The parts are then assembled and the product is ready to ship. The cost of publishing on demand this way versus producing hundreds of copies in advance and holding them in inventory is only about 15 percent higher. This particular product costs me about $20. I could save 15 percent of that, $3.50, if I produced, say, 300 of these things in advance, and tied up $6,000 in inventory for six months to a year at a time. To do that with twenty similar products, I'd have $120,000, more or less, permanently sunk into inventory, turning over sluggishly and slowly. By publishing on demand, I'm able to use all that money for marketing, and turn it over every month or so.

This is less important to me today than it was eighteen years ago, but for someone starting out, or someone who wants to offer a large number of titles to a specialized market, this can make all the difference in the world. Too many people make the mistake of investing months, even years, of effort in writing their information product, tie up all their money in a garage full of beautifully published books or audiocassette programs, and only then start wondering: Who will buy them? How will I reach these people? Where will the resources come from to do the marketing?

> **MILLIONAIRE-MAKER STRATEGY #41:**
> **LOOK FOR EVERY WAY POSSIBLE TO KEEP**
> **YOUR CAPITAL OUT OF DORMANT ASSETS**
> **AND INTO PRODUCTIVE ADVERTISING,**
> **MARKETING, PROMOTION, AND SALES EFFORTS.**

At various times, I have run businesses with as many as forty-two employees and as few as two; in 15,000-square-foot facilities, with a shower in the CEO's offices, a 1,500-square-foot facility with a refrigerator in the corner, and an office in my home, with both a shower and refrigerator just down the hall; with nothing more than a phone, answering machine, fax, and typewriter; with manufacturing facilities, with a retail storefront, with salesforces. Out of all that, I have arrived at several conclusions, for me. They may not all be just right for you, too, but they have proved important to me, so here they are:

1. Many people build businesses that are the antithesis of their desired lifestyles, and wind up trapped rather than liberated, frustrated rather than joyful, bored rather than creative, and often asset rich but cash poor. I have made this very mistake, and have spent years extricating myself from the results. I'm frequently tempted to make it all over again and have to fight the temptation.

2. Many people feel that they are not really "in business" unless and until they surround themselves with the physical trappings commonly and customarily associated with being in business, so they pile up overhead and fixed expenses to the detriment, not the facilitation, of achieving their most important goals via the shortest and most direct path.

3. The more your available financial resources, time resources, and energy resources are consumed by managing and taking care of and paying for things and employees, the fewer resources you have to devote to efforts that clearly and directly create sales, revenue, profits, and customers, and, secondarily, the less money you can extract from your business for yourself and your family. Generally, the more of your resources you liberate from things and employees and invest in productive advertising, marketing, promotion, and sales, the more money you'll make and the faster you'll make it.

4. The development and marketing of information products is a business endeavor that lends itself perfectly to avoid items 1 and 2 above, and to do item 3.

Can a Big Business Be Built with Simple Information Products and Direct Marketing? Meet the $200 Million Man!

My good friend Ted Nicholas started in the publishing business with a simple inspiration. Ted was a hyperactive entrepreneur who started a number of corporations; each time he incorporated, he was annoyed by giving the lawyers hundreds of dollars just to get a few forms filled in, usually by the lawyer's secretary. It occurred to him that this probably irritated a lot of other entrepreneurs, and for some people starting on really tight budgets who wanted to protect themselves through incorporation, it might even be too costly and stop them in their tracks.

A little research revealed to Ted that incorporation was actually very simple for most small business purposes, and anybody could fill out and file the forms. There was no requirement that a lawyer do it. Further, he found that there were significant tax, privacy, and other advantages from incorporating in Delaware, regardless of where a person lived and operated his business.

Ted wrote all this information down and turned it into a very simple, straightforward how-to book. He added all the forms needed to incorporate in Delaware, one blank set to use and one sample set completed as a model. Finally, he added the phone numbers and addresses of the incorporation offices and other contacts useful for incorporating in Delaware and every other state. He turned it into an 8½ × 11" 100-page book that cost him about a dollar to produce in quantity—although this same information could have been put in a number of different formats. (Today, form-your-own-corporation kits are commonplace, sold on computer diskettes, as books or manuals, or just the forms in an envelope. But at the time, Ted was plowing new ground.)

Ted titled his book *How to Form Your Own Corporation Without a Lawyer for Under $50.00*, and started promoting it with small classified ads in the *Wall Street Journal*, newspapers, and business magazines. From this very humble beginning, operating out of his living room, Ted went on to sell over 1 million copies of this book. In total, he sold over $200 million worth of thirteen different business books, manuals in three-ring notebooks, and reports he wrote, plus a number of other authors' products, before selling his company, Enterprise Publishing, to Dearborn Press, a New York book publisher, in 1992. You probably saw Ted's full-page ads for *How to Form Your Own Corporation* in airline and business magazines.

Ted has become something of a legend in direct-marketing industry circles. He is very much in demand as a lecturer at publishing and marketing conferences (including mine), and picks and chooses a consulting project now and again, but he spends most of his time at his retirement home in Switzerland, skiing, enjoying fine wines, traveling a little, writing a little, and relaxing a lot. The $200 million man is a very relaxed fellow.

If You Think Ted Nicholas's Success Is a Fluke *You* Could Never Duplicate, Think Again

Chase Revel started the business that ultimately became *Entrepreneur* magazine with classified ads, selling "Insider Reports" revealing the profits made in different types of businesses.

My client John Mortz earns a high five-figure annual income selling his reports, manuals, and courses about making money at home with your computer through classified and small display ads in a handful of magazines. John doesn't even have a single helper! His customers either mail in their orders or leave their orders with credit card information on John's voice mail. He publishes most of his products on demand, and ships from a Mail Boxes Etc. In my opinion, John could multiply his business ten times almost overnight if he devoted his full attention to it, but he enjoys doing consulting work in the computer programming field, so his information products business is still spare time.

Ted Thomas is a former airline pilot who got very rich making investments and organizing investment partnerships in single-family homes and apartment complexes during the last huge real estate boom in California and Arizona. Then, a dramatic change in interest rates and tax benefits tied to real estate yanked the rug right out from under his empire. One month, he was riding around in limousines, flying his own plane from city to city to buy properties, enjoying a millionaire's income and lifestyle; the next month, his properties were all in foreclosure and Ted was fighting to pay the rent on a cheap one-bedroom apartment. As a result of his crash, Ted learned a great deal about the hidden profits in foreclosures. Ted fought his way back to personal wealth by buying, trading, and reselling foreclosure properties. Gradually, he arrived at a system for making money that he believed anybody could learn and follow, which he wrote about in his first self-published book, which he began promoting with small ads and by speaking at real estate investment seminars. To avoid risking his own money, Ted developed unique joint-venture promotions with big names in real estate and investment training, like Howard Ruff and Robert Allen.

With virtually no investment of his own money, Ted quickly sold tens of thousands of his first book at the stiff price of $89 each. He expanded his information product line with several other books, audiotapes, and a home-study course all on foreclosure investing, another set of information products on negotiation, and, recently, yet another set of information products dealing with the how-tos of joint-venture marketing. His lowest priced item is $19.95, his highest priced $1,700!

The impressive success Ted has had with his own information products led him to contacts and working relationships with many other experts in this field, myself included, and in 1994 Ted hosted a three-day information marketers' conference in Las Vegas, with over twenty different speakers—including Ted Nicholas and me—over 500 people in attendance at an average of $200 each—$100,000 in registration fees—and, yes, he filled this conference through joint-venture marketing, without spending a cent of his own money.

My client Bob Burg is one of the top memory experts in the country; a master of easy-to-learn techniques for perfectly remembering names and faces, giving speeches and presentations without notes, and recalling phone numbers and addresses, facts, figures, statistics, even chemical formulas. He created his reputation through old-fashioned work: going out and giving speeches and seminars, at first for small businesses and sales groups and then gradually working his way up to large audiences and major corporations. Bob developed a number of audiocassette information products, including memory-training programs, vocabulary-improvement programs, and a course for salespeople, How to Create Endless Referrals. As a speaker, Bob sells over $500,000 a year of his information products personally. And his success with that method of marketing enabled me to obtain a contract for him with the Guthy-Renker Corporation, for his own TV infomercial.

From my own client base alone, I could give you dozens more examples, and I know of hundreds. But here's how to prove to yourself that you can do it, too: Pick up just about any magazine, and take note of everything from the classified ads to the large, full-page ads either directly selling an information product or offering free literature. Check issues of those same magazines at the library that are six months, a year, even years old—and you'll be able to find many of those same ads. Pick out a few dozen and answer them, and study the sales letters, literature, and information products you receive. You will soon see patterns that you or anybody could follow to achieve success in this field. Basically, if you know something that will be of interest to a certain group of people, and those people can be efficiently reached, you have the basis for this kind of business.

For Every Success I Tell You About, I Can Also Tell You About 100 Failures

Quite frankly, making a million selling information isn't as easy as I've probably made it sound so far. Oh, everything I've told you is true, and every component of success I've pointed out is valid, but there are a zillion little nuances in selecting the right markets, the right media, the right information, the right titles, well, the variables that have to be sorted out, tried, tested, and fit together to market each different information product profitably are almost endless.

Ted Nicholas figures that only six out of fifteen of his advertising campaigns for his information products have worked; nine out of every fifteen have failed. Gary Halbert says, "There's probably no human alive who knows more about making magazine advertisements pay off than Ted Nicholas." And I would agree. Yet, he fails nine out of fifteen times. What does that tell you?

Sometimes you hit the home run at your very first at bat. Recently, a partner and I created a brand-new information product, a new, untested full-page ad, ran the ad in several magazines, and had an instant, huge success—pulling almost three times ad cost with the product being sold in the ad, plus about 20 percent of those customers turned right around and bought our much-higher-priced, even-more-profitable information product. The numbers are still holding up, and this little business is on track to produce about $500,000 this year. Several months before this, for a client with a new, unusual information product, I had created a full-page ad that hit right out of the gate and now runs in about twenty different magazines a month to the tune of over $100,000 a month in advertising investment.

But, like Ted, I'll confess that more of my product ideas flop than succeed, more of my ads die than live, more of my infomercials bomb than score, and I'm wrong much more often than I'm right. And just about the time I start believing in my own genius, I confidently and optimistically give birth to a real clinker. Still, I have enough winners to more than make up for the losers, and that's why stepping up to the plate with some patience, persistence, and staying power is important in this business. It really is true, in this business, that just one good idea can make you rich.

From $100,000 in Credit Card Debt to a $200,000-a-Month Home-Based Business: How a Desperate but Determined Young Man Turned Failure into Success Virtually Overnight

One of the all-time best success stories in this category that I know of is that of Jeff Paul. There's always a student who surpasses the master, and I want to tell you about one of mine in detail, because his story includes an ideal model for anybody starting out in the information products business.

Jeff had been very successful as a certified financial planner at attracting new clients, but, for a collection of reasons I won't bore you with, he left the business and had no desire to return. But he knew he possessed valuable, important how-to information other financial planners would kill for. And Jeff was obsessed with the idea of creating a home-based mail-order business that would give him privacy, freedom, and a high income with minimal hassle. So he put the two together, wrote a marketing manual for financial planners, and attempted to sell it with ads in the trade journals read by financial advisers.

Unfortunately, he failed miserably.

Running ads, testing different ideas, fighting to get it right, Jeff managed to run up over $100,000 in debt on his credit cards. He moved his family in with his wife's sister and lived in her basement. When he and his wife, Peggy, first came to my seminar, they viewed it as a last-ditch attempt at finding out what they were doing wrong before declaring bankruptcy. They couldn't afford to join the other attendees in the restaurant; they snuck off to their room and ate peanut butter and crackers.

Most people, of course, would have given up. You can feel free to argue in your own mind whether Jeff is incredibly stubborn and persistent or incredibly stupid. The one tiny glimmer of hope that had brought them to the seminar was that they were doing some business. That month, they had sold $1,090 worth of Jeff's manuals. *Somebody* liked the idea and the product.

When I sat down with them and listened to what they were (and weren't) doing, it was obvious to me what needed to be done to turn his fledgling business into a winner. Now, I quickly want to disclaim genius, brilliance, or wizardry; it was just that I had already failed a whole lot more than Jeff had, and had lots of unsuccessful experience and a little bit of successful experience directly relevant to what he was attempting. So I gave them fifteen minutes of advice and sent them home. I'm going to let Jeff tell you the rest of the story in his own words:

> I'm writing this little contribution to Dan's book sitting at my kitchen table in my boxer shorts and T-shirt, where I have made an average of over $4,000 a day for the last two years. That's right: *$4,000 a day.* I have achieved the fantasy of making a ton of money from a home-based, easy, pleasant, information products business.
>
> Dan has told you that when I was trying to launch my business, I literally worked my family right smack into the proverbial poorhouse—actually living on a couch in a corner of my sister-in-law's basement. Now here's the unbelievable punch line: In just two years, I leaped from that basement to buying a $385,000 house with half down, no other debt whatsoever, money in the bank, a terrific daily income streaming in, and Peggy and I almost single-handedly run this business.
>
> After we went home from Dan's seminar and raced to implement the changes he suggested, our income exploded like a fireworks display. Here are the numbers, absolutely verifiable by my bank deposits: in the next month, October, we took in $13,400, in November, $26,200, in December, $49,800. In 1992 I took in over $1 million and I kept half as pure profit, after all my expenses. 1993 and 1994 have been even better.
>
> Let me briefly tell you what we were doing right, and what we fixed. First of all, having an information product solidly based on my credibility and track record, exclusively and specifically targeted to an enormous need and desire of a target market that I could reach easily and af-

fordably, that was all right. The biggest of my mistakes was trying to sell it in one step, with ads too small to get the job done, instead of using a multistep selling system that fit with my very limited resources and the nature of my product and market.

I quickly developed a series of marketing steps, beginning with ads that did nothing more than prompt a phone call to a recorded message. I also took my single product, a manual, and took it apart, reconfigured it into an entire collection of products—manuals, reports, cassettes, and forms. I started over again with an ad that cost just $138 and, by the third month, I took in over $50,000 from just $2,200 of advertising. I've since mastered such strategies as the "triple hoop advertising method," and "auto-pilot marketing," and learned how to get two-thirds of my profits from continuing relationships and additional sales to satisfied customers.

I became convinced that other people could learn and use my model to successfully sell just about any kind of information product, so I put it all down in a book titled *How You Can Make $4,000 a Day, Sitting at Your Kitchen Table, in Your Underwear.* Peggy hates the title. She says it's bad enough that I do sit around the house in my underwear, why tell everybody about it? But I find that revealing these things about myself helps people believe that they can do what I do. So we're now selling thousands of these books at $29.95 each as a second business.

If you read Jeff's story carefully, you were able to isolate a number of elements of a reliable, duplicatable formula for creating and selling information products successfully. Let me point out a few of the most important ones:

1. *Having a sound basis for your information products.* It is rarely a good idea to choose a subject area for products just because you think it is hot or timely. It is usually a good idea to choose a subject area you already have a background in,

considerable knowledge about, and can be reasonably considered an expert in.

2. *Having a properly selected target market.* Selection of the target market is at least half the battle. It needs to be a market you can reach easily, efficiently, and affordably; for example, if everybody in the target group reads one or two particular magazines. It needs to be a "starving crowd," a market that has demonstrated interest in and desire for the kind of information you intend to provide. It needs to be a market that has demonstrated responsiveness to direct-response advertising. All this requires research, and I've suggested methods and sources in chapter 13.

3. *Having a high enough price point to support necessary advertising and marketing efforts.* It is very difficult to make a profit by direct marketing a $19, $29, $39, or even $49 item these days. Personally, I would not undertake a campaign for anything priced below $99, and I'd prefer something priced higher. Jeff had to dissect his low-priced product, break it up into a number of separate products, and then reassemble those products into a new offer that had a much higher perceived value and commanded a much higher price (without a proportionately higher manufactured cost).

4. *Having a multistep marketing strategy.* Jeff has developed what he calls "triple hoop advertising": His prospects have to take three steps to prove their interest before he aggressively pursues them—they have to read his ads, call and listen to a lengthy recorded message, and record and leave their name and address. This describes the front end of his marketing system. The back end is made up of a timed sequence of sales letters and other mailings. While this is obviously more complicated than just running a one-step ad that asks for the order and makes the sale, this multistep approach is also much safer and reliable.

5. *Having an auto-pilot orientation.* By "auto-pilot marketing," Jeff means marketing processes that function by themselves without continuing physical labor. For example, collecting name and address information from prospects responding to your advertising via a free recorded message and voice mail

rather than by you or an employee answering the phone live. If most of your business is auto-piloted, you have more freedom and less overhead to worry about. Jeff has really mastered this business, and there is much to be learned by studying every little nuance of his operation. If you would like a copy of Jeff's book, refer to chapter 13.

6. *Having or quickly developing a back-end business.* The majority of big profits will come from the second, third, fourth, fourteenth, and fortieth sale to the same customer (back-end business), not from selling one product to one new customer after another (front-end business). The big profits are only in the back end.

Exploring New Frontiers in Information Products

As you work at developing back-end products, you'll be pushed into considering every possible media for packaging and delivering information. Three that tend to fascinate people the most are the much-ballyhooed 900 numbers, software, and newsletters.

900 Numbers

You have undoubtedly become aware of 900 numbers, the pay-per-call industry. Callers to advertised 900 numbers are charged by the minute or the call, at a flat rate, to listen to the message or, in some cases, converse live with a person. The information product is that recording; there's nothing to print, publish, manufacture, or fulfill. The long-distance carrier (AT&T, Sprint, MCI, etc.) and the service bureau that delivers your message for you through its equipment systems (capable of taking thousands of simultaneous incoming calls) each take a piece of the charges, but the biggest chunk of the charge revenue reverts to you, usually paid to you by the telephone company. The picture of creating a message once, advertising it, and strolling out to the mailbox once a week to get a big, fat check from AT&T is appealing, isn't it?

Unfortunately, the truth is that the overwhelming majority of successful, profitable uses of 900 numbers is limited to a very small number of businesses or products you might not want to be involved with, notably featuring hard-core sexual conversation (phone sex), soft-core conversation (confessions, chat lines, date lines), gambling tips, and psychic counseling. Once you go beyond those products, and uses by big nonprofit organizations as a means of collecting donations, the pickings get pretty slim for legitimate success stories.

There are also problems with message and advertising approvals from the long-distance carrier, and an even bigger problem with chargebacks: customers who do not want to pay their bill need only notify the phone company and they are let off the hook. They are always right, you are always wrong, and that's that. And this is a highly scrutinized, highly regulated business with frequently changing rules and regulations. Certain demographic groups, notably fifty years of age and older, are very reluctant to call a 900 number. Many companies, hotels, and other places have their phones blocked so that a call cannot be made to a 900 number. And all government offices have such phone blocks, the result of Pentagon employees running up huge phone bills calling 1-900-WHIP-MEE and similar lines. Some media refuse all advertisements including a 900 number. So there are a great many obstacles to deal with.

With all that said, however, there are successes. And enterprising, creative marketers are continually finding new and different ways to use 900 numbers profitably, either as a business or as a means of offsetting advertising costs in acquiring leads or customers. *Infotext* magazine (see chapter 13) regularly reports on these businesses. If you're interested in what works and what doesn't, you should subscribe to *Infotext*, and review a couple of years of back issues.

Personally, I have experimented with 900 numbers for several different purposes, mostly with unsuccessful results, and, in the few cases where I experienced success, it was not significant enough to justify continued investment and attention. I can tell you,

though, that the big secrets to profitability are media partners or
subsidized media. Since advertising is virtually your only expense, cutting that to the bone can make 900-number profits even
from unsatisfactory response. If you are putting out a newsletter
or magazine, distributing other information products, shipping
packages, or mailing catalogs in sufficient quantity, add a 900-
number advertisement with no added cost, or joint venture with
someone who can provide that media, so that you get to promote
the line with zero expense, and every call represents profit. Many
newspapers and magazines at least experiment with, and some
run ads with, 900 numbers for this reason.

Another way to profit from 900 numbers (or 800 numbers) is
by providing tele-services to your established customers. By serving established customers only, you minimize the nonpayment
problems and the costs of advertising and marketing the service.
You might have a frequently or regularly updated hotline of
timely information your customers can call. You might hold tele-
seminars or conference calls/discussions that customers pay to
dial into and participate in. These can be done through a 900 number, at a set charge per minute or per call, billed on their regular
phone bills, or via an 800 number, where they pay by credit card.

Information Products for the Computer Age

Software is an increasingly popular addition to information
products. *Entrepreneur* magazine now sells computer diskettes
with many of its business start-up manuals. Products like legal
forms kits, business letter collections, and time management systems are sold with diskettes or the diskettes are sold alone. My
client Larry Pino advertises and sells a product called The Desktop Lawyer, which is an entire collection of fill-in-the-blank contracts, agreements, forms, and form letters, all on diskettes.

Jeff Paul sells diskettes with the ads, direct-mail letters, and
other literature he teaches his financial planner–customers to use,
so they can pull those marketing documents up on their computers, make minor changes, and create their own literature inexpensively. Joke books for speakers are now available on

diskettes. It's probable that some aspect of your information belongs on diskette, and will be welcomed in that format by your customers.

Diskettes offer markups as good as or better than any other information product media, by the way. A diskette costing thirty cents to no more than a dollar to reproduce will sell for $19.95 to $200 or $300, depending on the content, use, and market.

Most recently, CD-ROM discs are becoming hot information products. There is a starving market; people with CD-ROM players are really hungry for more product, and seem to be buying discs on just about anything and everything. (A CD-ROM disc all about taking African safaris sold over 30,000 copies!) The reason there is such a shortage of product in this category is the barrier to entry. It has cost $100,000 to $200,000 to produce the master for duplicating these discs. Several entrepreneurs I know claim to have come up with do-it-yourself production technology that dramatically reduces that cost and is likely to spur an explosion of individuals self-publishing in the CD-ROM business in the next few years. I've included their information in chapter 13.

The Information Product That Provides Financial Security

Newsletters are, in my mind, increasingly attractive information products. Desktop publishing programs for personal computers and high-speed copying has made the production of newsletters easy and inexpensive. Including all costs, even postage, with a contribution to overhead, you can usually service a subscriber for $1 to no more than $2 per month; $12 to $24 per year. Even a low-priced newsletter, say $49 a year, offers as much as a 400 percent markup. And specialized-topic business newsletters can command $100 to $200 a year.

Publishing a newsletter keeps you in constant contact with your customers, at their expense instead of yours. Newsletters provide a great venue for self-promotion, advertising other products and services, bartering space with other publishers, and joint-venture marketing. You are forced to stay current on your specialty, pay attention to timely developments, and stay creative, and that's good discipline. Finally, the newsletter business allows you to stack up predictable renewal income, ultimately a significant measure of financial security.

The bad news, and the secret to the newsletter business, is that it is very hard to directly sell a newsletter subscription as your first transaction with a new customer. Newsletters are best sold to established customers who are already satisfied with other information you've provided to them and are set up to want a continuing relationship.

You might also consider an audio newsletter. The Guthy-Renker Corporation has been phenomenally successful selling subscriptions to Power Talk, a monthly audio series, to buyers of Tony Robbins's Personal Power Program from their TV infomercials. Power Talk subscriptions have been sold by direct-mail and by outbound telemarketing. Executive Book Summaries is a widely advertised, monthly audio series providing condensed versions of current bestselling business books for executives who don't have time to read.

Whether you "package" your information for sale on paper, on audiotape, on video, on a diskette, in a newsletter, or even as a 900-number recorded message, remember that the fundamentals of marketing remain the same.

MILLIONAIRE-MAKER STRATEGY #30:
CHOOSE DIFFERENT INFORMATION PRODUCT FORMATS
AND PRICES TO FIT THE TARGET MARKETS,
THEIR PRICE SENSITIVITIES, THE VALUE
THEY'LL DERIVE FROM THE INFORMATION,
AND OTHER FACTORS.

MILLIONAIRE-MAKER STRATEGY #31:
SELL THE SAME INFORMATION IN A NUMBER
OF DIFFERENT FORMATS,
AT A VARIETY OF DIFFERENT PRICES.

The same basic marketing principles and strategies that I teach repetitively are now sold in several books in the $10 to $20 price range, in audiocassettes for $99, in complete multi-media kits for $399 and up, in seminars with enrollment fees from $295 to $3,495 per person, and expanded on and updated in a newsletter at $199. Versions customized to different, very specific types of businesses are also sold. The variety in my product line welcomes the very casual person, the very serious student, the person who wants bare-bones, no-frills information, the person who wants to immerse himself in detail, the person who needs motivation and encouragement mixed with how-to nuts and bolts, the individual entrepreneur, or the corporate CEO.

Some products that are 90 percent the same are priced quite differently, based on their target markets. We sell a marketing kit targeted at a high-end, high-income profession for $200 more than a very similar generic kit that can be used by any small business owner. There is not a $200 difference in the product itself. There is a $200 difference in the value the user can easily perceive, accept, believe in, and get.

MILLIONAIRE-MAKER STRATEGY #22:
REMEMBER THAT WHAT YOU TAKE FOR GRANTED,
BECAUSE IT IS COMMON KNOWLEDGE TO YOU,
IS A REVELATION, A SECRET OF
IMMENSE VALUE TO SOMEONE
WHO DOES NOT KNOW OR UNDERSTAND IT.
DO NOT UNDERVALUE WHAT YOU KNOW.

I had a client some years ago, an ex-thief, who was a bona fide expert in all of the ways that employees in grocery and convenience stores steal merchandise and money from their employers. His information could easily save a single store owner $25,000 in ninety days to a year. When I met him, he was selling it all in a little booklet and four audiotapes for $50. When I gave him a makeover, that same information yielded two manuals, each priced at $29; two six-cassette audio programs with reference booklets, $199 each; a video series for employee training, $995; and a master course with all that plus interviewing, hiring information, materials, and honesty tests for $1,250. In the first year, his sales jumped from about $30,000 to $500,000. He was grossly undervaluing and poorly packaging his information. Simple corrections made a $470,000 difference.

HOW PUBLICITY AND PROMOTION CAN PRODUCE MILLION-DOLLAR BUSINESS BREAKTHROUGHS

Possibly the biggest challenge and most daunting expense for most entrepreneurs starting a business is acquiring customers. Is it possible to build a business with virtually no investment in advertising? Yes, and here's proof:

How Hellfire & Damnation Sauce Created Heavenly Profits

"If you can't stand the heat, get out of this catalog!" That's the warning given by Tim Eidson to his customers. He also quotes Mark Twain: "Part of the secret of success in life is to eat what you like and let the food fight it out inside."

In 1989 Tim and Wendy Eidson decided to get into the mail-order food business. After discovering that foods known to Tim from his Midwest upbringing, like sugar-cured hams and gooseberry pies, were already widely sold by mail, their attention turned to spices, then to hot things, and that's where they landed. Tim is a hot-foods fanatic and decided to go with his own passionate interest in business. The result: the Mo Hotta–Mo Betta catalog of foods that "put sweat on your brow, a tear in your eye, and a smile on your face."

With a $15,000 loan from a friend, and Tim's own ferreting out of products, Tim and Wendy got their first catalog produced and out to about 500 friends, acquaintances, and selected media contacts. Incredibly, they pulled a 25 percent response rate. And, since its launch, the business has grown at a rate of 300 percent a year. Today, the catalog has an annual circulation of 200,000 and generates nearly $3 million a year in sales.

But Advertising Failed to Heat Up
Mo Hotta–Mo Betta's Sales!

Tim and Wendy experimented with ads in magazines ranging from *Cooks* to *Spy*, and with direct-mail to rented lists, but were unable to get satisfactory results. Tim told *Direct* magazine: "We didn't really start to take off until people started writing about us."

Publicity became their one and only method of adding new customers. They targeted the food editors of every major newspaper in the United States, and began sending them samples of items like their Wasabi Chips, a Japanese snack heavy with a horseradish-like substance that sets your scalp on fire and drains your sinuses. Within a month, articles about the company, the catalog, and their products started appearing in newspapers. Thanks to clever product names like Hell in a Bottle, Hellfire & Damnation Sauce, and Satan's Revenge, Tim's offbeat catalog copy, and persistent contact with the media, Mo Hotta–Mo Betta has continued to generate lots of publicity.

"I Love You, You Love Me . . ."

Yes, it's that beloved-by-kids, occasionally annoying to parents, and even somewhat controversial giant purple and green plush dinosaur singing his trademark song and making millions for his creator.

Sheryl Leach was a typically underpaid schoolteacher on maternity leave when she got the idea to create educational videos for preschool children that would feature a child's "snuggly" brought to life. Originally, she planned to use a teddy bear, but switched it to a dinosaur after she and her two-year-old son visited a traveling dinosaur exhibit and she took note of his unusual enthusiasm for the creatures. The result, Barney the Dinosaur, is a friendly, happy modification of traditionally terrifying creatures made to look like a cuddly stuffed animal infused with life. He is a teddy bear in a dinosaur costume.

The first video, *Barney and the Backyard Gang*, was produced with a limited budget, and Sheryl ignored traditional toy manufacturers, trade shows, jobbers, and manufacturers' reps in favor of a unique grass-roots salesforce of mothers of young children, dubbed "Mom Blitzers," to descend on stores with enthusiasm, and convince the store owners to stock and display the videos.

The big breakthrough occurred when a Public Television executive bought one of the tapes for his four-year-old daughter. He was astounded by her enthusiasm for the jolly purple creature, and put Barney on the air, on PBS, in April 1992, and he was an instant hit. Public Television is a unique kind of publicity, by the way. PBS specials have made Covert Bailey into a household name in diet and fitness, and supercharged his career as a bestselling author. PBS specials made motivational speaker Les Brown famous.

Barney and Friends quickly became the most watched children's program on PBS, reaching a weekly audience of over 14 million viewers, two-thirds young children, one-third parents. Not only was and is all this exposure free, it is actually a business in itself, creating, producing, and providing the weekly programming. And what has it created? A dino-sized fad!

There are more than 700,000 members in the Barney Fan Club. More than 4 million Barney videos, 2 million plush toys, and 1 million books have been sold, with no end in sight. Barney's first record album went double platinum. As I was completing this book, Barney was appearing "live" in a series of twelve sold-out concerts at Radio City Music Hall in New York City, NBC-TV was finishing work on a one-hour, prime-time Barney special, and Sheryl and her partners were negotiating Barney's first movie deal. A continuing blitz of news releases to the media has helped sustain Barney as a hot commodity. One lesson here is to continually and frequently create and distribute news releases. There is value in persistence.

According to *Forbes* magazine, Barney ranks in the top forty entertainment industry money earners, with an estimated 84 million in the last two years. And even though Barney's marketplace power seems to be finally waning, he has delivered a dino-sized fortune to his creator, Sheryl Leach, and her production company, The Lyons Group. Sheryl is a millionaire several times over.

The happy creature has even sparked his share of controversy. Conservative Christian groups accuse Barney of sneaking up on kids with "New Age" and liberal political messages. The subject has even been debated on the Rush Limbaugh radio show! Sheryl insists there's nothing more to Barney than a "special friend" for children, invigorated by their own innocent imaginations, sharing universally acceptable ideas like good health habits, friendship, self-esteem, and respect for others. And none of this controversy hurts Barney in the least. Maybe it helps, as his fans rally to his defense. One thing is certain: Barney is a moneymaking force to be reckoned with!

MILLIONAIRE-MAKER STRATEGY #14: BREAK THE RULES.

To this day, Sheryl is convinced that Barney might have gotten lost in the shuffle and been ignored if she had taken the conventional approach of trying to place Barney with publishers or existent video producers, or sought distribution through established rep organizations. In an interview with the *National Enquirer*, she suggested: "If it's a new idea and you have limited resources, try an untraditional path. Go through the back door instead of the front door. And just never take no for an answer."

The Power of the Publicity Event

My friend Gary Halbert, consulting with Tova Borgnine in the very early days of her skin-care, cosmetics, and fragrance business, devised this outrageous strategy to launch her new perfume—an "unveiling," with the press and public invited, at a major Los Angeles hotel, advertised with the denial of a secret sexual stimulant included in the fragrance's formula.

"Tova Borgnine Swears Under Oath That Her New Perfume Does Not Contain an Illegal Sexual Stimulant!"

. . . screamed the newspaper advertisement's headline. Thousands caused a traffic jam and filled the hotel's ballroom to sample the new perfume and hear Tova deny the rumor of the aphrodisiac ingredient.

Another friend and colleague of mine, publicist Raleigh Pinskey, author of the book *The Zen of Hype*, used the event strategy to gain a ton of publicity for the Marilyn Monroe doll. When Raleigh was called to discuss the campaign, the toy company was only interested in coverage in the toy trade media—a basic who-what-where-when-why campaign on the project conception, development, and distribution coverage to boost orders at the upcoming toy fair. Ms. Pinskey showed them that instead of applying their efforts to the trade, they should approach the trade from the consumer angle. A back-door approach to the theory of supply and demand suggested that by creating a properly orchestrated rush for the doll on the consumer side they not only would generate orders from every possible avenue, but also might have a textbook legend on their hands.

Following Raleigh's advice, the manufacturer held back release of the doll, and led with a limited-edition, porcelain version outfitted with a real, although midget-sized, fur coat designed by a famous furrier, diamond earrings by a famous jeweler, and hair and makeup by a famous cosmetic artist to the stars. This limited-edition doll was priced at a whopping $5,000.

The porcelain Marilyn was kept under wraps until a much-publicized public unveiling: "She" arrived at New York's famous FAO Schwarz toy store in a Brinks armored car, and was escorted to her throne in the store by armed guards and Marilyn look-alikes.

When the truck arrived, the media was waiting, and they had attracted a crowd of curious onlookers. The event made all the TV news programs, the cover of the New York *Daily News*, a story in *Time* magazine, and, of course, all the trade publications of the toy, gift, and collectibles industries. The limited edition of $5,000 dolls sold out in a week. The regular doll had a successful tenure in toy stores nationwide. And the doll maker made a fortune.

> **MILLIONAIRE-MAKER STRATEGY #13:**
> **IT DOESN'T HURT TO BE A**
> **"CAPTAIN OUTRAGEOUS."**

Media mogul Ted Turner was dubbed "Captain Outrageous" by the press some years ago, and he has generated a huge amount of publicity by being outrageous. But the all-time queen in this category is Madonna. Arguably of little talent other than creating publicity by being outrageous, she's become a multimillionaire. Gary Halbert went down this path to promote Tova's perfume, and you can, too.

How I Deliberately Play at Being a "Captain Outrageous"

I applied the outrageousness strategy myself, incorporating a "No B.S." theme into two books and my personal promotion, beginning in 1993, with the publication of *The Ultimate No B.S., No Holds Barred, Kick Butt, Take No Prisoners, and Make Tons of Money Business Success Book.* The outrageous length and content of the title accomplished several important things. First, it got the book displayed face out, cover out (rather than spine out) in a number of bookstores, including a national chain. A relatively small publisher, like the publisher of my "No B.S." books (Self-Counsel Press), has to fight to get its titles stocked at all, then fight for shelf space. Second, it made the book leap off those shelves. Not knowing me from Adam's housecat, people were drawn to that title, grabbed the book, and told friends about it. Third, it generated considerable publicity, notably including being featured not once but four times in *Success* magazine and in *Inc.* magazine, countless newspapers, trade journals, and radio interviews.

One radio talk show host told me he hadn't read the book, but could ask me five good questions just based on the title. And he did: What do you mean by "No B.S."? . . . What do you mean by "no holds barred"? . . . What do you mean by "kick butt"? . . . and so on. We had a lively fifteen-minute interview and I responded to a number of callers.

At the American Booksellers Association convention, the publisher's staff wore and gave away buttons reading: "I'm A NO BS Entrepreneur" or "I'm A NO BS Manager," and we sent those buttons as well as desk placards to media contacts.

The success of the book prompted quick release of a second printing, packaged with two audiocassettes, sold off racks and counter displays, mostly in office supply stores and warehouses or club stores by the thousands. And, in 1994, the second book: *The Ultimate No B.S. Sales Success Book.* For this one's cover, I was photographed in a three-piece, pin-striped business suit, shirt and tie, sitting on an 1,800-pound, white Brahma bull ("Tiny"), out in the middle of the desert, at sunset. As you might imagine, I get a lot of comments about that book cover! And I use the same photo in a lot of my other promotion as a speaker and business consultant.

Yes, there have been critics and criticisms. But my theory is if you don't seriously offend at least one person a day, you're not saying or doing much.

How to Make a Million Just by Being Interviewed on Radio Talk Shows

The gurus of this unusual business are Joe and Judy Sabah of Denver, Colorado, students, subscribers, and friends of mine.

Joe and Judy have been interviewed on hundreds of radio talk shows, almost all from home over the phone, and have sold well over 21,000 copies of two of their self-published books just by giving out their 800 number, with zero advertising expense.

Joe and Judy self-published their first book, *How to Get the Job You Really Want and Get Employers to Call You*, as a result of Joe's experience helping his son create a direct-mail campaign to prospective employers that worked like gangbusters. Joe started out by calling radio talk show producers and booking himself, and then he devised more sophisticated, less arduous methods. He did all the interviews from home by phone, and simply, enthusiastically told the story of how he helped his son quickly and easily land a great job, then offered his book for $15 and gave out his toll-free 800 number. In the first year alone, Joe sold over 3,000 books.

Joe and Judy have been at this now since 1986, making book after book after book a profitable success just through radio talk shows. But their strategy will work for other types of products and businesses, too. In fact, they've helped people with a wide variety of products use radio talk shows as a primary marketing method.

There are over 700 general interest radio talk shows in Joe's database, and talk radio has enjoyed explosive growth in the past several years, with no end in sight. And every show's hosts and producers are in constant, sometimes frantic, search for good, articulate, interesting, entertaining, or controversial guests who can hold listeners' attention and, on call-in shows, make the switchboard light up.

My friend Al Parinello has been the host of his own nationally syndicated radio talk show and has interviewed over 3,000 people. He has owned and operated radio stations, worked on the development of both Nickelodeon and The Movie Channel, appeared as a guest on many talk shows, and has pioneered the use of radio infomercials. *TV Guide* called him "one of a new breed of space-age super salesmen." Al gave me this great example of the power of radio talk shows:

I once interviewed an insurance sales representative on the topic of retirement planning. This is not an especially scintillating topic and I was worried that things would get a little boring. But, happily, the guest surprised me. He revealed that the Social Security Agency is making serious mistakes in more than 10 percent of all accounts, and he gave out his 800 number for listeners to call, and he would give them, free of charge, the form they needed to get an analysis of their account from the government.

The radio station's phones rang off the hook and we had a lively and interesting program.

The insurance agent got more than 1,800 calls to his number, gaining 1,800 potential clients' names, addresses, telephone numbers, and interest. Needless to say, this led to selling a lot of insurance.

And this was just in New York, on a local radio station.

This same strategy could be used nationally, with interviews on hundreds of stations, to sell books, newsletters, or other products related to seniors' finances and retirement activities.

Getting on radio talk shows is mostly a matter of persistence and grunt work. Here are the steps:

1. From one of a number of sources, including those listed in chapter 13, you need to compile your own target list of stations, program managers, and talk show hosts. You may have a geographic preference and only want to go after stations in certain states or cities. Maybe you want to start with small stations or maybe you only want to target the 100 biggest stations in the country. Using criteria that match your particular objectives, you create your target list. For my most recent effort, for certain reasons, I went after only those stations of a certain size that carried the Rush Limbaugh syndicated program.

2. You begin communicating with a basic news release, simple letter, flyer, or even a postcard. Joe Sabah uses an oversize postcard printed on a garish, eye-catching colored stock. I prefer the more traditional approach of a brief cover letter

and a one-page news release sent in an envelope. It is increasingly common to send the news releases by fax, too.

The cover letter should identify who you are, the name of your company or organization, the book or product or idea you are publicizing, and why you and it will be of great interest to the station's listeners. The news release, like a news article, needs to be real news. It should have an attention-getting headline. The host or producer will be looking for the news angle, for what is provocative, predictive, or timely.

Some people also include other support materials, such as suggested questions for the interview, reprints of articles about them from major media, book covers or actual copies of books, or reference letters from other radio station hosts to document that they are good guests, give good interviews, and attract lots of callers.

Instead of sending all this material at one time, an effective alternative strategy is to dole it out in a series of several mailings a few days apart.

3. Many hosts and program producers are diligent about examining all of this material, and if they believe your topic will interest their listeners and light up the switchboard, they will book you. However, the door never slams shut all the way, so if you fail to stimulate their interest with the first contact, you can keep trying. Here's where the grunt work comes in: Nothing beats getting on the phone, calling, talking briefly with these people personally and then, if you get them interested, immediately faxing or FedExing your materials to them again. This takes a lot of time, patience, and persistence. You'll play a lot of phone tag. You'll call at bad times, find out when you can reach a person, and have to call back. But it can pay off. After one recent mailing campaign to 130 stations, we called them all, persevered in getting through to the right individuals, and found that fewer than twenty remembered receiving and looking at the mailing. But, with the phone contact and sending the material again and following up by phone again, we've gotten very good results.

4. If at first you don't succeed, try again, with a new angle. Let's say you publish and market books, manuals, and videos about

training dogs. One publicity campaign directed at radio might present you as "The Dog Trainer to the Stars." You might time this with the Academy Awards, so you could be interviewed about Hollywood celebrities' pets. In November, you might go with a "Warning to Parents About Buying Dogs as Gifts for Your Children." Different hosts and producers will respond differently to different presentations at different times.

An Entire Business Built on Talk Radio Interviews

Now, here's the most inventive strategy I've ever heard: A client of mine, who has asked not to be named, and requested that I "disguise" the nature of his product and business revealed this to me. I give it to you here as a "disguised" but nonetheless valid example.

Bob M. is a former pro athlete who develops, manufactures, and markets a couple of unique health-related products. He picks a market, and gets just one health food store or sporting goods store in a well-known mall to take an inventory of his product on consignment for just one week. He puts the inventory in entirely at his expense and splits the sales with the store fifty-fifty. Then he does a blitz of every local radio and TV talk show he can get on, talking about his career, ideas, and products, and tells everybody when he'll be at that store to meet them in person. Each day, he does interviews during the day, spends the evening at the store, and finishes the week by being at the store on Saturday.

In most cities, he'll do at least $20,000 in business during the week. He's done as much as $50,000 in a single week. After the split with the store, travel costs, mailings to the media, and his cost of product, Bob keeps about 20 percent of his gross; $2,000 on $10,000. He usually works two weeks out of every month and takes two weeks off. Last year, he grossed over $700,000, and kept about $130,000 net. Now, he's busy cloning himself with four spokespersons who will have territories, buy from him, and split their profits with him, so this year he may do as much as $3 or $4 million in gross sales and retain profits of as much as $500,000.

Can You Profit by Getting on National TV Programs?

Why not you? My one-time client, now good friend, Lee Milteer, a motivational speaker and author, persistently sent her press kits, literature, books, and tapes to the hosts and producers of all the major TV talk shows in the United States and Canada, and advertised repeatedly in *The Radio & TV Interview Report*, a trade publication read by producers.

She was invited to appear on *The Dini Petty Show*, the Canadian counterpart to *The Oprah Winfrey Show*, to talk about goal-setting, visualization, and stress relief. From that single interview, she instantly sold over $40,000 of her audiocassette products via an 800 number and captured thousands of customers for later follow-up. And she was so well received she was ultimately hired by the show to make regular guest appearances. In total, her appearances on *The Dini Petty Show* alone have probably been worth over $250,000 to her in direct business, not to mention the indirect benefits.

Two appearances on *The Phil Donahue Show* by Gloria Pitzer, known as the Recipe Detective, literally made her business. Gloria Pitzer publishes a homemade, simple newsletter of recipes, featuring do-it-yourself versions of famous food products like Kentucky Fried Chicken, McDonald's special sauce and French's mustard. On *Donahue*, she demonstrated how you could duplicate these products with simple ingredients, 'very cheaply, right in your own kitchen. She gained thousands of paid subscribers to her newsletter with zero advertising expense. And keep in mind this was not somebody with television experience, influential contacts, the help of a costly publicist, or any other advantage you lack.

And Al Parinello told me about Elysa Lazar's appearance on ABC's *Good Morning America*. At the end of her interview, she offered a copy of her newsletter, *The Mail-Order Shopper*, for $1.50 . . . and a few days later, somebody called her from the post office and asked what she wanted done with her mail. Puzzled, she told them to deliver it to her home just as they always did. In the next few days, her mail carrier dragged bags of mail onto her porch filled with 70,000 checks for $1.50!

Every Smart Entrepreneur Uses Publicity at Least Occasionally

Most of the entrepreneurs I use as examples throughout this book include deliberately sought and created publicity in their mix of marketing tools and methods. Bob Stupak of Vegas World (see chapter 2) has played blackjack against a computer for a $500,000 wager on television (and won), made the largest recorded single bet on a pro fight in Las Vegas ($1 million), run for mayor, risked going on *60 Minutes*, invented weird casino games like Crapless Craps, and is now building the nation's largest tower—all with publicity clearly in mind.

Guthy-Renker (see chapter 8) employs a public relations firm to make sure Bill or Greg gets quoted by just about any media reporting on infomercials. The result? Coverage in everything from *TV Guide* to *Fortune*. Harv Eker (see chapter 11) aggressively sought publicity for his fitness product stores, with the goal of attracting the attention of larger, acquisition-minded corporations.

Tom Doyle at Gripping Solutions (see chapter 3) gives away free sets of his mountain bike grips to competitive racing teams and editors, writers, and columnists of bicycle magazines. The result has been positive articles in most magazines and powerful quotes from those articles that he is able to use over and over again in his advertising. Joseph Cossman (see chapter 3) was an absolute master at using publicity and publicity events to promote his products throughout his career. A publicity stunt he staged for his Spud Gun toy, in conjunction with the toy show in New York City, deluged the city with potatoes from farmers all over the nation and nearly got him arrested—but it made the lowly Spud Gun the blockbuster hit of that trade show.

> **MILLIONAIRE-MAKER STRATEGY #35:**
> **EVERYBODY CAN FIND A WAY TO USE PUBLICITY.**
> **DO NOT UNDERVALUE PUBLICITY**
> **BECAUSE YOU DON'T BUY IT.**
> **DON'T IGNORE IT JUST BECAUSE IT**
> **TAKES EFFORT TO GET. IT *IS* VALUABLE.**

At the very least, every smart entrepreneur includes publicity in his arsenal of promotion and business-building methods. A few rely on it exclusively to build their businesses. Publicity is commonly used to generate ''hot'' leads for follow-up by mail, by phone, or in person, like the insurance agent on Al Parinello's show did. Publicity is also commonly used to launch new products without lots of advertising, like Raleigh did with the Marilyn doll. But there are many other ways to use publicity, and you should carefully consider how each one might apply in your situation.

The Bottom-Line Secrets to Publicity: The 5 *P*'s of Publicity

Whether you decide to go the do-it-yourself route and be your own publicist or you invest money to hire and use a public relations agent, the bottom line is the same. There are five keys to creating publicity and to getting publicity opportunities:

1. *Be predictive.* The public loves predictions of the future. Every new year psychics like Jeanne Dixon get enormous amounts of publicity by issuing their predictions about world and national events, celebrities' lives, and other subjects. Talk radio is frequently populated by experts, authors, researchers, and seers making predictions about everything from the stock market to the end of the world. In the business environment, author Faith Popcorn became famous on the strength of her predictions about consumer behavioral trends.

One of the most popular financial newsletters in America is Mark Skousen's *Forecasts and Strategies*, and the word *forecasts* is not in its title by accident. Mark is an experienced talk show guest and media manipulator, and he has learned the power of being predictive. In a speech in October 1989 at an investment conference, Mark announced to 500 investors and attending media, "The Berlin Wall will be torn down," and discussed the implications of that with investors, even though his prediction was greeted with laughter and cynicism. One month later, the Wall was down. Over the years, he has made a number of equally impressive predictions that have come true. (He has also made a number that haven't, but public memory seems to be remarkably forgiving of seers.)

2. *Be provocative.* In my book *The Ultimate Marketing Plan*, I cite being boring as the #1 Marketing Sin. I believe your customers, clients, and prospects will tolerate just about anything and everything but being bored. Well, this is doubly true with publicity. The public has a very short attention span, and the media knows that grabbing and keeping the public's attention requires the provocative. Doug Casey got tremendous publicity some years back for his book *How to Profit from the Coming Economic Crisis.* People instantly wanted to know—What crisis? When is it coming? How should I prepare?

One of the most consistently successful users of radio talk show appearances for marketing purposes is Laura Corn, author and self-publisher of the book *367 Questions Every Woman Should Ask Her Man.* It is an obviously provocative topic. Regardless of who you are, whether you're a woman or a man, married or single, young or old, it is almost irresistible. Aren't you instantly curious about what these questions are? Why should women ask them? What will men answer?

Barbara DeAngelis, another popular author, seminar leader, infomercial star, and repeat guest on daytime talk shows, talks about "the five secret ticking time bombs in every intimate relationship." When she brings this subject up, everybody understandably wants to know what those ticking time bombs are. Do I have any ticking away in *my* relationship?

Authors of "conspiracy" books about topics ranging from John F. Kennedy's assassination, Chappaquiddick, and Elvis's death to the Clintons' past financial machinations and the president's alleged sexual liaisons easily get publicity. A large segment of the population has immense, easily provoked distrust of all authority, and most people prefer an explanation for a tragedy, rather than chalking it up to happenstance. With these tools working for them, conspiracy theorists can always command attention.

Tax protestor, author, and speaker Irwin Schiff boldly states that all income taxes are voluntary and enforced collection of income tax is unconstitutional. On talk shows, he challenges anybody to bring him a section of the tax code that directly contradicts him. The *fact*—usually revealed by Irwin himself—that he has twice been put in prison and done time for tax evasion does not dissuade tens of thousands of people from buying his books and attending his seminars!

Inventors of safety products, advocates for and against gun control, self-defense instructors, and manufacturers of burglar alarms all have found publicity opportunities thanks to the increasing public concern about crime, and those who take especially provocative positions are media favorites.

3. *Be public.* By this, I mean mainstream. For example, it's much easier for, say, Laura Corn to generate lots of media publicity than for me to do so; she deals with sex, love, and relationships, and nothing is more mainstream than that. I deal in business topics, of interest only to a limited percentage of the population. As a result, most of the publicity I do get is in business, financial, and trade publications, which does serve my purpose. But I don't fit with Donahue, Oprah, Geraldo, or even *Today* very well. If you want that kind of major media exposure, you have to find a way to be mainstream.

4. *Be a personality.* Broadcast media just about require that you have a dynamic or humorous or intriguing personality. Matthew Lesko writes huge directory-type books like *Info Power.*

He appears frequently on *The Larry King Show* and does phenomenally well, because he is a very excited, excitable, entertaining personality. Larry is virtually guaranteed a good show. Diet and exercise guru Richard Simmons is regularly welcomed by Leno, Letterman, and Regis and Kathie Lee because he is a character.

5. *Be persistent.* Every show's producers' and hosts' interests, concerns, and needs change on a day-to-day basis. This week, nobody is interested in the child psychologist who has invented a new line of educational toys that combat gender and racial prejudices. Next week, a group of girls sue a public school system for sexual harassment, and *The Phil Donahue Show* is going to put together a panel of experts to comment on juvenile sexual harassment. Now that psychologist could be hot.

　　Most shows' staffs maintain extensive files of press kits and materials that are submitted to them. I have several clients who have been called to appear on talk shows a month or even a year after they submitted their materials. But the smartest tactic is to frequently send new information, articles, press releases, and other materials to a target list of media contacts.

11

YOU MIGHT MAKE YOUR MILLIONS FASTER BY SELLING OUT THAN BY STAYING IN

There's an old joke about the U.S. government social worker making the rounds of the Indian reservations, settling on this sleepy chieftain, and trying to motivate him, believing if she could get him into "the program," all the others would follow.

"We would pay for you to go to school and get an education," she told him.

"Why would I do that?" he asked. He was sitting on a creek bank, under a shade tree, with a fishing pole stuck in the mud, its line dangling in the water.

"So we could help you get a good job with a good company."

"Why would I want that?" he asked.

"Well, if you stayed there and worked hard for thirty or forty years, you'd be able to retire."

"Why would I want to do that?" he asked.

"So you could spend the rest of your years relaxing, doing whatever you wanted to do."

"Doin' that now," the chief answered.

Of course, the distinct difference is to retire with money or without it, and, as the comedienne Totie Fields said, "I've been with money and without, and with is better." I believe that the great dream of many entrepreneurs is to develop their business to a certain point and then have some giant corporation pay them a king's ransom for it, so that they can walk away and travel the South Seas, join the senior golf tour, or whatever. But few entrepreneurs set out from the very first moment of enterprise to make that happen. T. Harv Eker did that. And he asked himself the question, *Why take a lifetime to get this done—why not do it fast?*

From Biz Dunce to Biz Whiz after Just
Seventeen Lessons

T. Harv Eker is one of the most interesting guys I've met on the speaking circuit. He's a Canadian transplanted to sunny San Diego, where he occasionally puts on what he calls a "Street Smart Business Boot Camp," and more frequently, there and in other cities, he supervises "Street Smart Business Schools," modeled somewhat after the Dale Carnegie Courses.

I was a guest speaker at one of these camps the weekend after Thanksgiving in 1993. There were about 400 students there, and Harv had pulled together a diverse group of speakers—Robert Allen, author of *Nothing Down*, the get-rich-in-real-estate bestseller; Ted Thomas, a joint-venture marketing expert; Ann Boe, a networking specialist; Dr. Wayne Dyer, a metaphysical philosopher; and me. Ironically, the most interesting speaker of all was probably Harv, because he told a story I'd never heard before, that of very deliberately setting out to create a business for the sole purpose of selling it for big money as quickly as possible.

These days, Harv's students call him "The Biz Whiz," but for quite a while he was more of a biz dunce. Harv bumbled his way through seventeen different businesses in a relatively short period of time. "It stands to reason that if I have gone through that many businesses, only a few of them survived for any duration," Harv admits, "but the more businesses I owned, the more lessons I learned. In 1983 I decided to get married and settle down. I also decided to get rich, once and for all. In order to stay rich, I realized that I had to do things differently than I had in the past."

Stay Away from Great New Ideas

In analyzing what had caused him the most grief in his past business ventures, Harv determined it was making brand-new, inventive ideas work. That was risky, costly, and time-consuming. This time, he went in search of a business that was already proven, apparently poised for explosive growth, but nonexistent in his own area. And Harv found the home fitness retail store. "These stores were flying high in Los Angeles," Harv recalls, "but nobody'd even seen one in Toronto, or anywhere in Canada, for that matter."

By transplanting what was already working in one place to another place, Harv took a very valuable shortcut. In this instance, he had to be a good observer, astute enough to study the already successful business and understand the principles and strategies that were causing its success, but he did not have to be a successful inventor or innovator.

Pay Attention to Trends

"I looked at a number of successful, potentially transplantable businesses and business ideas, but I settled on the fitness equipment store because it was in sync with not one but a number of societal forces likely to insure its success. They were: (1) a general increase in health and fitness product sales; (2) an increase in the senior population, the increase in life expectancy making people over fifty-five the fastest-growing group (and these people needed to exercise more but weren't eager to go to health clubs); (3) what Faith Popcorn (author, *The Popcorn Report*) identified as the "cocooning" trend—people staying at home; (4) the increase of home-based businesses, so people had to stay home; (5) women in the workplace [with] full-time careers and families, [who had] no time to hang out at the health club; and, (6) the public's passion for convenience."

Harv did a good job. In fact, these trends have held up over the long haul, supporting the current proliferation of home fitness equipment advertised and sold via TV infomercials, such as those with "Body By Jake," Joe Montana, Joe Piscopo, and Jane Fonda, via pervasive magazine and newspaper advertising, and in every department store, discount store, and warehouse club. Once there was only NordicTrack, now there are hundreds. Whether this trend holds up four years from now or not, I can't predict. (You may be reading this book many years from now and say, Piscopo who?) But the trends Harv spotted did hold up long enough for him to become a millionaire.

Determine to Build a Salable Asset, Not Just a Business

The biggest thing Harv did differently is that he viewed his new business as an asset, in his words, "similar to a house or piece of real estate." He set the goal of cashing out as soon as he could get $1 million for the business, and a companion goal of doing that as quickly as possible, and that altered the way he approached developing and running the business.

In April 1984 Harv opened Fitnessland, the first fitness equipment store in Canada. "Most people look at businesses as vehicles for income," Harv explains, "but my research indicated that businesses get bought for a combination of reasons and, often, income is of the least importance. There's gross sales, proof that the business is expandable and has potential to grow with the new buyer's capital and ideas, public recognition, [and] market share. These are all important values to build into the property."

With that in mind, Harv systematically reinvested virtually all the profit in growing the business's number of outlets and gross sales and in creating a business image that was even bigger than the business itself. The first year, Fitnessland had $850,000 in sales with a whopping $220,000 in profits, but in two and a half years, Harv expanded to ten stores with $7 million in gross combined—but only $36,000 in profit. The money was reinvested in creating a first-class, franchise company–like appearance, in securing territorial exclusive marketing rights to certain products, and in generating as much media publicity as possible.

Harv reasoned that these assets would have greater importance and value to a larger company acquiring his business than would a higher profit number. And he believed that the image and publicity would attract suitors.

He proved right on both counts. The first break came when Fitnessland's advertising attracted the president of the Canadian operating division of the H. J. Heinz Corporation to the store to buy a treadmill. He was so impressed with what he saw, he started asking questions about the business, then told Harv that Heinz was on the lookout for businesses they felt they could grow into giants. Heinz's acquisitions people were soon involved, and Harv had a serious, qualified suitor on his hands.

Creating Competition: You're More Desirable When More Than One Wants You

"Once I had the Heinz deal in play, I sent out letters to health-related companies in Canada. Basically, I told them a U.S. company was starting negotiations to buy my business, but that I would prefer to keep the company Canadian owned, if I could." Harv adds, "And I had a detailed business plan to show them, forecasting expansion to 100 stores in Canada and in the United States, making the argument that capturing this market quickly was important."

Soon Harv had seven other companies in the game, all considering acquiring his company. In subtle ways, he let each discover the others. This motivated Heinz to move quicker and more aggressively than it ordinarily would. It took a year—a long time for the impatient entrepreneur, but a short time for a major corporation to complete an acquisition—and Harv Eker cashed out of Fitnessland for $1.6 million, achieving his original goal of being an "after-tax millionaire."

"I am absolutely sure," Harv says, "that you can never

make as much money running a business as you can selling a business.''

MILLIONAIRE-MAKER STRATEGY #17:
CLARITY OF PURPOSE.

If you really pin people down, even business owners and entrepreneurs, you'll find most cannot clearly and concisely enunciate exactly what they are trying to accomplish this year, in three years, or in five years. They're running around playing what I call ''blind archery,'' and that's a pretty difficult, even dangerous game. Harv Eker had a very clear, concise understanding of what he wanted to get done through his business in five years or less: Walk away an after-tax millionaire. This definite objective then governed all of his creative thinking and decisions.

In a similar fashion, most of my activities these days have something to do with the objective of accumulating 5,000 paid, happy, renewable, renewing subscribers to my marketing newsletter. I choose or turn down speaking engagements, joint-venture opportunities, and other projects based on whether or not they'll make a contribution to achieving this goal. My entire mail-order business is conceived as a giant funnel leading to newsletter subscription. Being focused on one, clear beacon like this makes navigating the waters on a day-to-day basis a lot easier.

MILLIONAIRE-MAKER STRATEGY #19:
ARE YOU SURE YOU WANT TO BE A PIONEER?

A lot of pioneers get shot full of arrows and die. As Harv learned through his seventeen lessons, it is often a lot smarter and surer to find a way to build on the solid foundation of something that is already a proven success, rather than creating something entirely from scratch.

I am a huge believer in creative theft. When I work as a consultant with one kind of business, I identify some principle of success, some strategy that is working for them, then take it and apply it to a second client's business in a different field, where the strategy is new. And while I'm doing that, I can find something that the second client's industry is doing and "steal" it to apply in an entirely different industry. You can certainly do the same thing for yourself. Harv found a successful idea he could transplant geographically. You might do that, too. Or you might do as I do—find an idea you can transplant from one type of business to another.

**MILLIONAIRE-MAKER STRATEGY #24:
PAY ATTENTION TO DEVELOPING TRENDS.**

The idea is to see "leading indicators," not "trailing indicators." For example, in 1993 the percentage of young people who smoke crept back up, fast-food and junk-food consumption increased, and the total number of people entering formal weight-loss programs declined. If you look at all the advertising you see for weight-loss products, fitness products, and health foods, you might find those facts hard to believe. But you'd be looking at "trailing indicators"; the 1993 statistics may be "leading indicators." In fact, some highly respected trend analysts are using such facts as the basis for predicting a dramatic drop in sales for the health- and fitness-related businesses in the next three to five years.

Faith Popcorn, a legendary trend predictor, has coined the name *pleasure revenge reaction* for this; in other words, the public has deprived itself and tortured itself to lose weight and get better bodies, many have only gained back weight lost through grueling or expensive diets, and now all that frustration is going to play itself out in people saying, "The heck with it. If I want a banana split, I'm having a banana split."

In 1984 Harv saw a lot of current and leading indicators that led him to believe in a coming boom in health and fitness, and he was right to the tune of $1 million. If he were looking at today's indicators, Harv would be making very different choices about the type of business to develop.

**MILLIONAIRE-MAKER STRATEGY #42:
SMART INVESTMENTS IN BUILDING VALUE.**

If you are interested in developing and then selling a business, or merging with a big, "deep pockets" parent, or even going public, it's important to understand that net income is rarely the most important success factor. The business owner only using his business as a means of earning a living can (and, usually, should) make the bottom-line profit number his top priority. But the entrepreneur with a bigger vision needs to build value, not just create income.

Why Would a Ketchup Company Buy a Chain of Fitness Stores, Anyway?

About eight years ago, I went to a seminar on how to sell your business put on by The Geneva Corporation, and one key principle I heard there for the first time has since been of immense value to me. Here it is:

> People and companies buy businesses for *their* reasons,
> not yours. Their reasons for buying not only have nothing
> to do with your reasons for selling—they'll have little to
> do with the reasons you think somebody ought to have
> for buying your business.

This means that you need to think very creatively when positioning a business for sale and selecting and courting buyers. You have to crawl inside their minds and try to understand their reasons for buying.

With this in mind, I've since sold two of my businesses for considerably more than they were worth on paper. For example, I sold the manufacturing division of a company I owned to a direct competitor, with the appeal to him largely based on two things: the merging of my customer base with his existent operation, so he had instant added sales but no added costs, and the value to him of removing me from the marketplace as a competitor. Now, the truth is, he was whipping me in that competition. He was better financed, had better and newer technology, and lower prices. But I was a skilled, tough marketer and a thorn in the side of his business. His company spent money on certain kinds of advertising that would not have been necessary if I was out of the picture.

This value had nothing to do with the reasons most people think businesses are bought. For example, the equipment was a nonissue because of the differences in technology. The inventory was also a nonissue. Even the business name and identity were unimportant. In this case, two assets were involved: customers and elimination of an annoying competitor.

Synergy often plays a role. I recently sold a specialized division of one of my publishing companies to a small firm providing services to the same unique niche market. For me, this was one of a number of product lines and markets. For them, it was their only market, and because all their resources and energies were targeted at that market, it cost them less to promote additional products than it did me to deal with it as one of many opportunities. For me, it had actually become almost a nuisance, and it was being neglected because of that. They almost immediately doubled the sales of the product line they acquired from me because of their more dominant presence in the market and laser focus on the market. I made the argument that the business would pay for itself and be worth much more to them than to me. That was true, and it was the basis for a deal satisfactory to both of us. In Harv's case, it so happens that the H. J. Heinz Corporation was already in health-related businesses—notably, they owned Weight Watchers International—and had targeted this as a big area of opportunity they wanted to exploit.

There's also an ego or arrogance factor at work when an entrepreneur's business is bought by a big company. The big company's executives believe they are much smarter and more capable than the entrepreneur "who got lucky." This is why gross is much more important than net in most cases. Rapid growth of gross screams "potential." But when they look at the low net, they chalk it up to the entrepreneur being an inept manager. "If we bring in a good management team," they reason, "we can plug all the profit leaks. Cut fat. Reorganize." Well, there's nothing wrong with letting them be arrogant. Go ahead and be humble and dumb. And cash the check.

It's axiomatic, by the way, that the arrogant big company buys the entrepreneur's business, ruins it, and destroys it in a matter of years. Gerardo Joffe, one of the real wizards of mail-order, built up a terrific business with Haverhills. It was a fore-runner to The Sharper Image. He sold it to Time/Life for a lot of money, and they ruined it. After they killed it completely and his noncompete agreement was void, Joffe started all over again and built up a Haverhills-clone called Hennikers.

The big company that I sold my company's manufacturing division to really got the short end of the stick in the deal, mostly thanks to their own arrogance. First of all, they devoutly believed I was wrong about many of my approaches to the business. Second, they believed they could dictate their policies to the customers if they became the only game in town. Third, they overestimated the value of the entire market. What they didn't understand was the "smallness" of most of the clients in this particular market, so when they tried to force high minimum production runs on them and took away the "babying" personalized service we'd been giving them, they lost 80 percent of the customer base over a couple of years. Other smaller competitors sprang up and took that business away from them. They still did okay. They made a profit on the deal. But nothing like they thought they would, because ego and arrogance got in their way.

How to Get the Very Best Deal Possible When Selling Your Business

I've violated most of these steps in the two deals I've done for myself, because I was willing to knowingly trade off dollars against speed and simplicity. In one case, I initiated the talks, flew to the candidate, pitched his executives, and closed a deal, all in two days. Could I have gotten more money by handling this differently? Almost certainly. But I did get a good, if not great, deal, and I was a motivated seller, with little opportunity or urge to appear otherwise. If you want maximum money, though, these are the six steps followed by those who get top dollar:

1. *Do not need to sell.* In most negotiations, the person most willing to walk away from the table wins. If Harv had not found a buyer, his $36,000 in profits could easily have gone to $50,000 or $60,000 the next year, $100,000 the year after that, and he could have gone on living very well running his chain of stores for years.

2. *Demonstrate tremendous potential.* I think one of the best cases that can be made to a buyer bigger than you are is that your business could grow much bigger, much faster if it only had the capital and credit, and be much more profitable if it only had the buyer's expert management.

   Imagine having a farm that is productive, has good yields per acre, an immaculate appearance, and a good water supply, and you are farming it with a mule-drawn plow. Along comes a big company that owns and manages thousands of farms, has every imaginable piece of modern, automated equipment, efficiency experts, soil analysts, and so on. That's how Harv's business must have looked to Heinz, and he did nothing to interfere with that picture, and did everything he could to paint it. "What I've done is good—but imagine what you could do!" is the message.

   During the last couple of months that I was writing this book, Ron Perelman invested a very large sum of money in the Guthy-Renker Corporation. Ron Perelman is, according to *Fortune*'s 1993 list, one of the 101 richest people in the world, a billionaire and then some. The terms of the deal allowed Bill Guthy and Greg Renker to immediately take out capital gains and enhance their personal fortunes, provided the company with more capital and much more credit, and gave them special access to other assets and opportunities within Perelman's "empire" (such as Revlon; SCI Television, a chain of TV stations; Marvel Comics; Genesis Entertainment and New World Entertainment; TV production and syndication companies; and Coleman, the outdoor equipment company), and let them retain control over their company. Why would Ron Perelman make such a small deal, in comparison to his other interests, and give them such a good deal? He must believe that the synergy between Guthy-Renker and his other interests is so great, and that the potential for growing Guthy-Renker is so great, that just by adding his resources to the mix, the value of Guthy-Renker and his piece of Guthy-Renker will massively multiply.

A lot of what went on in making this deal was, from Guthy-Renker's side, "Look at everything we've done, but here's what we could do if we had . . ." and from Perelman's side, "What they've done is good, but imagine what they could do if they had *a*, *b*, *c*, *d*, and *e*, and we've got all that."

3. *Attract suitors, don't seek them.* There are certain business situations where proactive, very aggressive action perversely works against you more often than not. In my business, selling consulting and speaking services, you have to learn how to attract clients, because if you go right at them, they run away. The same thing's true in finding buyers or major investors for your business. If you go after them, you'll probably drive them away or, at the very least, you'll diminish the price you'll be able to negotiate and get.

Capitalizing on having the first retail fitness product store in Canada, Harv did everything he could to create massive amounts of publicity for his company. He also invested in creating a corporate image that made his business appear bigger and more sophisticated than it actually was. He deliberately assembled elements likely to be attractive to a big corporate buyer or investor. He carefully constructed a giant magnet and let it attract.

When I look at Guthy-Renker's deal with Ron Perelman, I see the payoff of several years of substantial investment in public relations and publicity that served no direct purpose as it was being done. To a much greater degree than the owners and leaders of the other companies in the infomercial industry, Greg Renker sought out and welcomed opportunities to appear on TV programs and be interviewed by and quoted in print media, ranging from *TV Guide* to the *Wall Street Journal*. He employed a professional publicist. He frequently generated news releases. He got a lot of "spotlight time" as the organizer of this young industry's trade association, the National Infomercial Marketing Association.

Also, at the expense of certain and quick profits, Greg and Bill passed on infomercial projects likely to create negative publicity and regulatory agency interference. While other infomercial companies got hit with FTC, FDA, and state attorney generals' actions and adverse publicity over some of their most successful but arguably sleazy shows, Guthy-Renker took a higher road, a more conservative approach, and invested heavily in thorough documentation of advertising claims made in their shows, and served as the primary force raising the production standards of the entire industry. There is no doubt they could have pulled greater short-term cash profits out of the business with a different approach. But just like Harv Eker learned, bottom-line income is not the most important factor in attracting favorable attention from much larger corporate entities.

4. *Be patient.* If you are going to design and develop a business with the intent of selling it in order to walk away a millionaire or better, I think you have to plan on a five- to ten-year time frame. Harv Eker got there in just shy of five years, Guthy-Renker in about seven. And as I look at similar examples, I see that five- to ten-year time frame appearing consistently.

It also took Harv about a year to get from Heinz's decision to a done deal. And that required considerable patience! But most big corporations cannot and do not move with the speed the small entrepreneur is accustomed to. Most multi-million-dollar deals will take months to get done, and will come apart and be put back together a couple of times along the way.

5. *Ignore conventional evaluations of what your business is worth.* "My accountant," Harv Eker said, "told me that the maximum my company was worth was $400,000." Harv got $1.6 million. The accountant's assessment will always be based only on what *is*, using formulas of asset value if liq-

uidated, and some multiple of net earnings. And all that is textbook correct. But it is not the way to walk away wealthy. And, contrary to all the textbooks in the world, it is not the way big deals are done in the real world.

In the movie *Butch Cassidy and the Sundance Kid*, Paul Newman is ridiculed for riding a bicycle and talking about the modes of transportation of the future. His character says, "The whole world's looking at things through bifocals while I'm lookin' through binoculars." Accountants use bifocals. You need to get your buyer looking through binoculars. "That vision thing," as President Bush used to say, is very important.

6. *Start by asking for a lot more than you want.* Actually, many smart negotiators believe in forcing the buyer to make an offer without first naming their price. Harv told me, "Ignoring the $400,000 my accountant told me about, I sat quietly and waited until the people at Heinz named a figure. It was $1 million. And I was ecstatic, but I calmly told them I wasn't interested in selling unless it was so clearly worth my while that I couldn't say no." Harv then set his price at $2 million. They settled at $1.6 million.

The most important thing that Harv did, though, was to create a bare minimum scenario below which he knew he would not go. "There is no way," Harv said, "that I was leaving that business unless I was an after-tax millionaire." In most cases, I believe in starting with a number double my acceptable price, and with a strong rationale for that doubled number.

Earlier in this chapter I mentioned Gerardo Joffe. He started his first mail-order business, Haverhills, in 1966 and sold it in 1971 to Time, Inc., for 18,000 shares of stock with a market value of $56.50 each. When he started Haverhills, he had no mail-order experience. He had a background as a mining engineer, no training or mentors in the field, little capital, and he was over forty years old at the time. He learned as he went along.

One key thing he did, early on, was to lock in on the idea of developing a mail-order business that would be desirable as an acquisition for a large company, so that he could sell it and walk away a millionaire. Like Harv Eker, his intent all along was to create a salable million-dollar asset. In his book *How You Too Can Make at Least One Million Dollars in the Mail-Order Business*, he points out an advantage of developing a mail-order business for sale. "By the very nature of the mail-order business, you will create multimillions of advertising impressions. The name of your firm, even if still on the modest level of $1 to 2 million in sales, will have large public recognition and will almost have become a household word. Those in charge of acquisitions in major corporations will know about you and your business. They will have formed a positive impression about your business and will be predisposed toward acquiring it."

When Gerardo Joffe sold Haverhills to Time, he admits to being in negotiations with three other firms also interested in buying Haverhills. Like Harv Eker, Gerardo Joffe constructed the right kind of magnet, then he let it do its job of attracting suitors. And you cannot chalk it up to luck. After his noncompete agreements with Time expired, he started an almost identical business, Hennikers, which he sold to another mail-order company in 1979. Later, he started and built a third similar company, Russells, which he sold to an airline in 1982. He then purchased the name Haverhills back from Time and started another company. There is a model here that you can follow.

12

THE ULTIMATE MILLIONAIRE-MAKER STRATEGY

In this book, I've exposed more than 100 different categories, types, and applications of businesses useful in taking any good idea and turning it into a fortune, highlighting forty-five different Millionaire-Maker Strategies. Unfortunately, many people will read this book with bifocals and blinders on, hastily tuning out anything that doesn't immediately seem directly and specifically relevant to their particular product, service, or business, as they see it at this moment. That's a big mistake. If you've gone through this book quickly, saying "*that* doesn't apply to me" and "*that certainly* doesn't apply to me," my purpose here is to send you all the way back to the beginning with a new perspective.

How an "Ordinary," Small Hotel Gift Shop Became a $5 Million-a-Year Business

Bob Neumann became a hotel owner sort of by accident. In 1985 Bob opened a small, specialized gift shop, Grizzly's Gifts, in the lobby of the Anchorage Hotel. His family had been in retailing for years. He saw the transition of Alaska's economy from oil to tourism, so opening a gift shop featuring Alaskan artifacts, crafts, gifts, and souvenirs was a natural evolutionary event.

Then Bob was dragged into the mail-order business. In his gift store, among the Eskimo-made knives and blankets, salmon, seal oil candles, and scenic postcards, a funny little item, "Canned Alaskan Earthquake," became the star. (This is a cleverly labeled can that grumbles and shakes when it is picked up, and rocks from side to side if picked up and quickly set back down.) People began writing in and calling in to buy more of these Earthquakes, and Bob responded by first advertising that product, and then developing a catalog to make follow-up sales to his lists of customers.

Then a little crisis hit. Grizzly's Gifts' home, the Anchorage Hotel, was a famous landmark visited by most tourists coming through the city. In its heyday, the Anchorage had hosted the likes of Will Rogers, Walt Disney, and President Warren Harding. Unfortunately, the hotel had lost its luster. In fact, it had become a run-down dog housing prostitutes and drug addicts. Its decline led to its going on the block. Bob was certain that anyone buying it would want to get rid of the few stores housed there, including his and his parents'. Finding another prime downtown location would be prohibitively expensive, if not impossible. So he bought the hotel in 1988. He and his wife then invested $250,000 and a lot of hard work in turning the fleabag into a classy, European-style hotel. The result has made Grizzly's Gifts prosper wildly; the store has doubled in size and, during the prime tourism summer months, employs forty-five people. The mail-order business has grown from 5 percent to 15 percent of all of Grizzly's Gifts' business, and its sales have jumped from $200,000 in 1985 to nearly $5 million in 1994! And that doesn't include the hotel business, which is also a raging success.

Admittedly more reactively than proactively, but nonetheless courageously and effectively, Bob Neumann has utilized the ultimate Millionaire-Maker Strategy: synergy. By fitting three businesses together in a synergistic manner, the whole is much more valuable and successful than the sum total of the parts. Synergy takes pieces and multiplies rather than just adding.

> **MILLIONAIRE-MAKER STRATEGY #43: USE SYNERGY!**

Succeeding in the Success Business
with Synergy

By now, you have probably seen a Celebrating Excellence catalog. If you haven't received one in the mail, you may have seen them bound into airline magazines. The Celebrating Excellence catalogs, now called Successories, feature plaques, posters, paperweights, awards, notecards and stationery, and T-shirts all sporting motivational, inspirational, customer service–oriented or management axioms, and books, gift books, and cassettes. Many of these are upscale products. The posters, for example, are beautiful original photographs—called "Action Art Lithographs"—that sell for as much as $69.95 each.

The original catalog operation started small, as an extension of a printing and graphics business based in Lombard, Illinois. Its owner, Mac Anderson, himself a devout believer in good old-fashioned positive thinking, used his graphics company's capabilities to create the business's first products. After seven years of building his catalog business, Mac opened his first Successories Store, with the idea that it would act as a showroom, corporate headquarters, and base of operations for his outside salesforce calling on businesses in the Chicago area. But the foot traffic, off-the-street sales at the 1,700-square-foot store were pleasantly surprising. In 1991, its first year, the store exceeded $700,000 in sales.

Mac then opened three more company-owned stores, and quickly put the power of duplication to work through franchising. Today he owns over 80 franchised stores in U.S. cities, rapidly growing toward his goal of 250, plus distributors in Australia, Holland, Ireland, Saudi Arabia, Singapore, and South Africa. The stores benefit from constant, massive national advertising of all the locations through the millions of catalogs mailed and distributed via airline magazines and gift catalogs during the year. And almost every store has an outside salesforce, utilizing the store and the catalog, but focusing on corporate quantity buyers of awards rather than individuals.or small businesses.

The catalogs provide fundamentally free advertising for the stores. The stores utilize the same catalogs as their own. The revenue from the stores and the existence of the distribution pipeline make it easier for the company to continually invest in new, original product development. The stores' salesforces secure business from a type of clientele that might never walk in and buy off a store shelf, but, while doing so, automatically promote the stores and the catalogs, so that contacts they make but do not convert to clients may later visit a store or shop from a catalog. The outside salesforce and the advertising for the stores by the catalogs serve to make the store franchise a more certain, reliable success for the franchisee. Catalogs × Stores × Salesforces = Millions.

The overall success of this three-pronged synergistic strategy is impressive: over 100,000 corporate customers, including Xerox, AT&T, 3M, and Ford, and total sales in 1993 exceeding $13 million. At the end of the first quarter of 1994, Celex Group, Inc., the parent of Successories, Creating Excellence, and its publishing arm, Great Quotations, announced record sales and earnings, featuring a whopping 129 percent increase in sales compared to the same quarter in 1993. Barring any unforeseen disaster, Celex may as much as double in size over the next two years.

The MiniConglomerate Philosophy

I have long encouraged my clients to view their businesses and business opportunities very differently from most. If you start asking people "What business are you in?" or "What do you do?" you will usually get answers that impose very limited definitions on their activities. They box themselves in, mentally and otherwise. A person who owns a chain of jewelry stores, for example, may answer, at worst, "I'm a jeweler" to, at best, "I own a chain of jewelry stores." But those very definitions preclude consideration of such opportunities as creating an outside salesforce to sell recognition jewelry to businesses or a catalog business or importing pearls from the South Seas or putting up-scale engraved gift kiosks in the same malls where they have stores or creating a "wedding store" or "wedding catalog" or a travel business specializing in unique honeymoon trips or . . .

There is a difference between being focused and being re-stricted. One of my most frequently dispensed suggestions is that you focus on the customer. You'll recall my other references to TCV, Total Customer Value. Once you come to grips with the fact that the single biggest expense of business is acquiring a new customer, then it becomes evident that it can be easier and more profitable to grow by offering more products and services to the customers whose trust you have than by only searching for new customers. Then you can fit that idea together with other synergy. If you put two consumer service businesses together under one umbrella, you not only halve the cost of acquiring customers, you share fixed and operations expenses in order to create better bottom-line profits.

You might also focus on the product. Disney was the first to ask the very smart question: Since our characters are eagerly licensed by manufacturers of all kinds of merchandise that sells by the multimillions in all kinds of stores, why don't we have our own products sold in our own stores? Now it's hard to walk into a mall anywhere without finding a busy, very profitable Disney Store. Their success awakened a sleepy Warner Brothers to the neglected product value in their characters, and now equally successful Warner Brothers stores are proliferating like crazy. Both Disney and Warner also have thriving catalog busi-nesses, and their catalogs promote their stores.

When I coauthored the "Be Your Own Boss" products with Tony Robbins, Fran Tarkenton, and *Entrepreneur* magazine's columnists, and the TV infomercial that promoted this product, I interviewed Beverly, a bright, dynamic lady who had used *En-trepreneur*'s Business Start-Up Guides to launch her gourmet muffin shop in Atlanta's The Underground. She had a successful shop, baking and selling muffins, including many unusual muf-fins from her own recipes, such as "Meal-In-A-Muffin" items like spinach and mushroom muffins. The store, however, wasn't as net-profitable as she had hoped, so she was thinking about other ways to make money when a local Wal-Mart executive, who liked her products, asked if she could supply the area Wal-Mart stores with packaged muffins to sell.

She did *not* say (or think): I'm not in the wholesale bakery business. She said yes. And, instantly, she *was* in the wholesale bakery business. Initially, she marshaled a night shift of workers who produced muffins for Wal-Mart stores right there in the store. But soon, the demand of Wal-Mart and other stores she added to her clientele forced her to expand to a larger muffin "factory" in a lower rent area. The last time I talked to her, her wholesale business was much bigger and more lucrative than her store.

Odds are, in your current business or the business you're about to create, you have or will have an asset, be it the customers, the product, or something else that could and should serve as the basis for very creative synergistic expansion. Here are a few quick tips for recognizing it and exploiting it:

THINK BIGGER!

Most big businesses began as small businesses. There's no reason that you can't expand, duplicate, diversify, combine, etc., and turn your small business into an exciting, growing business.

THINK BROADLY!

Don't define your business too narrowly. Give yourself mental creative room to maneuver and to respond to new opportunities.

THINK LEVERAGE!

What is your greatest asset? Is it a loyal, highly responsive clientele? Is it store traffic? A phenomenal location? Your product or products? Whatever it is, how can you get more leverage from it? How can you better exploit it? Mickey Mouse was a cartoon character, of use originally only in short cartoons for movie theaters. But that same asset has been leveraged via comic books,

books, videotapes, movies, cartoons, clothing, toys, theme parks, a cable TV network, and on and on and on.

THINK SYNERGISTICALLY!

What elements can you combine under your single roof or umbrella that multiply rather than just add to the value of your business?

A Final Word from the Author

There is a reason that people choose the United States of America over every other nation in the world. They wait patiently and fight persistently to gain entry legally. They risk their lives to sneak in illegally. They come across the harsh, dark desert; they row here on rafts. This has been going on since the beginning of America, and it will go on as long as we remain a true free-enterprise society. Why? Because of the Great American Dream.

And they can have it. This remains a place, just about the only place, where anybody can set and achieve virtually any goal, regardless of where they start, regardless of the particular obstacles they carry with them, and that goal can certainly include turning their ideas into a million dollars or more. This book is intended, in part, as a reaffirmation of the availability of The Dream.

I tell people that I am woefully unqualified for every business activity I'm involved in, every success I have achieved. I'm one of the highest-paid advertising copywriters and marketing consultants in the field, yet I never attended college and never had any formal education or apprenticeship in advertising. I'm a very successful professional speaker who routinely earns $10,000 to $25,000 per speech (in fees plus educational materials sales), and who has shared the platform with a long list of celebrities, including two former U.S. presidents. But, when I was a kid, I stuttered almost uncontrollably, I got a C in high school speech class, I never had any formal training, I never so much as went to a Toastmasters meeting. I've made millions of dollars with my ideas, and helped my clients make hundreds of millions of dollars. And now I've written this book. I hope my example is encouraging, my ideas helpful, and that you've enjoyed and profited from reading this book.

Summary List of Millionaire-Maker Strategies

#1 Diversify in marketing, to fully exploit
Total Customer Value.

#2 Diversity is the opposite of laziness.

#3 Gutsy (not wimpy) marketing.

#4 Keep it **simple.**

**#5 Turn anger and resentment against an enemy
into enormous opportunity.**

#6 Sell time.

#7 Provide the customer with an **exceptional guarantee.**

#8 Stake out a **leadership** position.

#9 Being Alert!

#10 Even if yours isn't a true service business, **add and
emphasize a service component.**

#11 Creative combining can create huge business
breakthroughs.

#12 Plus-ing.

#13 It doesn't hurt to be a "Captain **Outrageous.**"

#14 Break the rules.

#15 Others may criticize you—**listen to your customers
first and most.**

#16 Tweak, tweak, tweak.

#17 Clarity of purpose.

#18 Consider priorities other than the fastest-possible growth.

#19 Are you sure you want to be a pioneer?

#20 Everybody has **assets of experience and empathy** that should be considered and valued when choosing business activities.

#21 Turn your passions into profits.

#22 Remember that what you take for granted, because it is common knowledge to you, is a revelation, a secret of immense value to someone who does not know or understand it. **Do not undervalue what you know.**

#23 If you're going to invent, **consider markets first.**

#24 Pay attention to developing **trends.**

#25 Uncover hidden assets and opportunities.

#26 If you don't ask, you can't get.

#27 Think big!

#28 Get others to do your selling for you.

#29 **Acquire customers for free** any time, any way, every time, and every way that you can.

#30 Choose different information product formats and prices to **fit the target markets,** their price sensitivities, the value they'll derive from the information, and other factors.

#31 Sell the same information in a number of different formats, at a variety of different prices.

#32 Develop vertical businesses within your business.

#33 **Private labeling** is a fantastic way to get massive distribution fast, with no advertising and little marketing expense.

#34 Create your own **toll booth.**

#35 Everybody can find a way to use **publicity** in
your business.

#36 You *must* find ways to use the power of television. It is
the most powerful force in American society.

#37 Take full responsibility for the success or failure of
your ideas.

#38 Success breeds success.

#39 Properly **value information,** especially when gained
through failure.

#40 Selling brilliantly won't make you a million if you're not
buying smart!

#41 Look for every way possible to **keep your capital out of
dormant assets** and into productive advertising, marketing,
promotion, and sales efforts.

#42 Smart investments in building value.

#43 Use Synergy!

#44 Discovering and using "formulas."

#45 It ain't over 'til it's over.

Summary of Key Strategies for the Eight Best
Ways to Make a Fortune in America

In chapter 1, I gave you an overview of the eight best ways
to make millions with your ideas. Throughout the book, you've
seen and learned from people and businesses exploiting these
opportunities. Here's a summary of the key strategies and ideas
you hopefully found and considered in each of these eight areas
of opportunity.

1. Turning ordinary businesses into extraordinary money machines

- Charge premium prices *and* deliver premium value.
- Lead your marketing with irresistible offers.
- Create extra profit centers.
- Diversify your marketing efforts.
- Continually listen to your customers—react and respond.
- Deliberately build on customer loyalty.

2. Exclusively control your products and businesses

- "Have" the market, then get the product (the reverse of most people's approach).
- Pick products (and businesses) using proven criteria with your greatest interests.
- Negotiate for limited, carefully defined exclusive rights in a way that is a win-win for you and the manufacturer or other party granting the rights.
- Remember, if you don't ask, you don't get!

3. Profiting from service businesses or service components incorporated into other businesses

- Think big! (Service businesses do not have to stay small.)
- Design services that solve people's most vexing problems.
- Design services that save people time.
- Specialize.
- Follow your talents.

4. Duplicate and multiply

- Systemize; the foundation of fortunes made through duplication is a rock solid system of one kind or another.

- Duplicate your knowledge, methods, and attitudes in others.
- Turn your business or moneymaking system into a "business opportunity in a box."

5. Get involved in the exciting world of direct marketing

- Bypass middlemen and complicated distribution—go direct to the end user and build relationships with your consumers.
- Use your marketing as a means of collecting data about your customers.
- Test, test, test.
- Tap into others' databases and established customer relationships.

6. Turn information into millions

- The most in-demand, most-consumed commodity of our time is information.
- Packaging and selling information, with emphasis on publishing-on-demand, gives you enormous financial leverage.
- If you know "how to," you have the basis for a profitable information marketing business.
- If you're not going to be in the information business exclusively, at least incorporate information products and information marketing in your other business. Plus your other product(s) with information components.

7. Publicize!

- Publicity is so powerful it can even build businesses with no other proactive advertising or marketing. This fact tells you that you must make it part of your mix of business-building methods.

- Find a way to inject an element of outrageousness into your publicity.
- Talk radio is booming all across America—tap into it!

8. Combining

- Very few fortunes are made one and only one way. Just about every time an idea makes millions, a number of these ways have been creatively combined.

13

HOW TO USE ARISTOTLE ONASSIS'S BIGGEST BUSINESS SECRET: THE MILLION-DOLLAR ROLODEX

Late billionaire Aristotle Onassis said that the secret to success in business is to know something nobody else knows. Along these lines, one of the most frustrating, time-consuming, and often costly challenges of turning ideas into profits is finding the right contacts, vendors, resources, information, and knowledge.

Over the years, I have built up quite an arsenal of resources. I have already sifted and sorted through thousands to arrive at the relatively small number that I rely on repeatedly. In this chapter, I pass those on to you. You might think of it as having a million-dollar Rolodex on your desk, as it has cost me at least that much to assemble, and could be worth more than that to you now, just in time saved.

In contacting these sources, it will be of benefit to let them know you read about them in my book. In many cases, you will get discounts or other special considerations as a result.

Important Notices About the Million-Dollar Rolodex

1. Although every effort has been made to ensure the accuracy of the listings provided here, the very nature of publishing a directory is that information will be out of date and incorrect even before the

darned thing gets into print. So, neither I nor my publisher can accept any responsibility for inaccuracies in these listings. I will remind you that your library's business librarian can be incredibly helpful in tracking down directories, companies' new addresses and phone numbers, and all sorts of information.

2. Being included in these listings does *not* constitute endorsement by me or by the publisher. In many instances, I've listed suppliers and contacts I've had very good experiences with, but that's just no guarantee that you will have the same kind of experience and feel the same way. Consider what I've done here as a very valuable shortcut in your shopping and information-gathering activities, but do not consider it some kind of warranty. It is not. You are an adult, responsible for your own decisions. Caveat emptor.

3. Because time will elapse between the assembly of this information, its publication, and your obtaining it, all offers must be subject to change without notice.

CONTENTS OF THE MILLION-DOLLAR ROLODEX

PRODUCT SOURCES
Where Can I Look for Exciting,
Promotable Products?
How Can I Find Products and Make
Important Contacts in the World of
Import/Export?

MAIL-ORDER AND DIRECT MARKETING
How Can I Get My Product(s) Sold by Catalogs,
Stores, and Other Established

Distribution Channels?
How Can I Get on and Make Money from
the Information Superhighway?
How Can I Learn More About the
Infomercial Business?
How Can I Get My
Products Sold on the Home Shopping Networks?

MARKETING
How Can I Get Celebrities as Spokespersons
or to Endorse My Products?
How Can I Create Positive Publicity
for My Business?
How Can I Get My Ads Placed at
the Best Rates Possible?
How Can I Put Together Super-Powerful
Direct-Mail Campaigns for My Business?

INFORMATION PRODUCTS
How Can I Get More Help Developing and
Marketing Information Products?
How Can I Produce My
Audio- and Videocassette Products?

BUSINESS MANAGEMENT
How Can I Get Set Up to
Accept Major Credit Cards from
My Customers?
How Can I Get the Best Prices and Assistance
With My Printing and Publishing Needs?
How Can I Handle Fulfillment of
the Orders I Receive?
How Can I Most Efficiently Sell by Phone
to My Inquiries and Customers?

ADDITIONAL ASSISTANCE
How Can I Best Build My Knowledge,
Make Contacts, and Discover Opportunities

Where Can I Look for Exciting, Promotable Products?

Publications

Publicity Express
2646 Appian Way #31K
Pinole, CA 94564
510-669-2202

Publicity Express regularly publishes and distributes *Hot-Picks*, a compilation of "hot," new, unusual products in search of publicity and marketing. A typical issue describes hundreds of products.

American Manufacturers Directory
c/o American Business Directories
5711 S. 86th Circle
Omaha, NE 68127

115,000+ U.S. manufacturers by size, type of products, SIC codes, geographical locations, etc. Includes key contacts.

Modern Plastics Encyclopedia
McGraw-Hill
1221 Ave. of the Americas
New York, NY 10020

5,000+ plastics processors, converters, manufacturers, makers of prototypes, and related suppliers.

Thomas Register of American Manufacturers
212-290-7277

Thomas Register is probably the most complete national look at manufacturers and their products. It is quite expensive to buy, but is available at most public libraries.

Mail-Order Product Guide
B. Klein Publications
Box 8503
Coral Springs, FL 33075
305-752-1708

1,500+ manufacturers, importers, and distributors eager to distribute their products through mail-order companies.

Directory of High Discount Merchandise Sources
B. Klein Publications
Box 8503
Coral Springs, FL 33075
305-752-1708

1,200+ sources of products offered at unusually high discounts. Lists organized by product category.

Close-Out Traders & Promotional Merchandise Guide
Empire Communications Corp.
5818 N. 7th St. #103
Phoenix, AZ 85014
800-223-7180

Introduction to the close-out, liquidation, distressed merchandise industry, including thousands of sources and trade shows; instructions on how to buy at ten to thirty cents on the retail dollar; how to use deeply discounted promotional merchandise to promote your business.

Classified ad sections *USA Today*, *Wall Street Journal*, and major city newspapers (*New York Times*, *Los Angeles Times*)

In one issue of the Sunday *New York Times*, I counted over 200 different ads placed by manufacturers, importers, liquidators, inventors, and other sources of an incredible variety of products, all seeking distribution, marketing assistance, help with mail-order, salesforces, or quantity buyers. In that same issue, there were twenty "Want to Buy" ads from various marketers, exporters, etc., looking for particular kinds of products. And, under "Business Connections," another fifty ads including new inventions and products, businesses seeking investors, investors seeking new opportunities, advertising media offered at discounts, and much more. The diligent entrepreneur regularly reading the classifieds from a dozen cities, plus *USA Today* and the *Wall Street Journal*, could find a true wealth of product sources and opportunities.

Government Inventions for Licensing
c/o National Technical Information Service, Dept. of
Commerce
5285 Port Royal Rd.
Springfield, VA 22161
703-487-4732

A publication that describes government-owned patents and inventions that private entrepreneurs can license on a royalty basis for certain purposes.

Trade Shows

I am a big advocate of attending trade shows as a means of finding new products, ideas for products you might create, and important contacts. And there are trade shows in every imaginable business category.

Annual Trade Show Directory
Forum Publishing Company
383 E. Main St.
Centerport, NY 11721
516-754-5000

Lists and describes over 1,000 U.S. trade shows.

Worldwide Tradeshow Schedule
Glahe International, Inc.
1700 "K" St. NW #403
Washington, DC 20006
202-659-4557

Free list of 110 major international trade shows.

Directory of Conventions
Bill Communications Inc.
355 Park Ave. South
New York, NY 10010
800-253-6708

14,000+ national, regional, state, and local meetings, conventions, and exhibitions.

Tradeshow Week
Reed Reference Publishing
121 Chanlon Rd.
New Providence, NJ 07974
908-464-6800

How Can I Find Products and Make Important Contacts in the World of Import/Export?

Publications

Info-Trade
4201 Cathedral Ave. NW 902E
Washington, DC 20016
202-966-8706

Leading research organization in the export industry. Publishes detailed manuals listing export by geographic market and by industry.

Directory of U.S. Importers
Directory of U.S. Exporters
The Journal of Commerce
445 Marshall Street
Phillipsburg, NJ 08865

These publications track the details of over 50,000 trading firms and 140,000 decision-making executives. If you need to select and reach importers or exporters, these specialized publications may be the resources you need.

Hong Kong Exporters Directory
International Business Directories
1300 Main St.
Springfield, MA 01101

450+ companies offering over 8,000 products for export from Hong Kong/import to the United States.

Ron Coble
Coble International
1420 Steeple Chase Dr.
Dover, PA 17315

Ron publishes a variety of directories, how-to manuals, home-study courses, and newsletters dealing with import/export. An inexpensive starter item is his Import/Export Success Tape for just $14.

American Register of Exporters & Importers
38 Park Row
New York, NY 10038

Made in Europe
Box 174027
D-6, Frankfurt-am-Main
West Germany

Commercial News USA
U.S. Dept. of Commerce #1310
Washington, DC 20230
202-482-4918

This publication is distributed by our government to more than 250,000 contacts in foreign markets. Advertising is as inexpensive as $400.

How Can I Get My Product(s) Sold by Catalogs, Stores, and Other Established Distribution Channels?

Product Distribution

Infomercial Products Network/Lombard Management Inc.
12015 Mora Dr. #4
Santa Fe Springs, CA 90670
310-944-9494

A network of manufacturers' representatives and sales organizations that can take new products or products first sold via direct-response advertising/direct marketing into retail stores throughout the United States, Canada, and overseas markets. They are well known for taking products that have sold via direct-response TV commercials to the store shelves.

Manufacturers Agents' National Association/Directory
Box 3467
Laguna Hills, CA 92654

Approximately 10,000 members: independent sales agents representing manufacturers on a contract basis.

Direct to Catalogs, Inc.
6600 Coffman Farms Rd.
Keedysville, MD 21756
301-432-4410

Brokers/representatives exclusively to the catalog industry.

Santa Barbara Promotions, Inc.
133 W. De La Guerra St.
Santa Barbara, CA 93101
805-962-8456

Places products in credit card statements, catalogs, and other print advertising promotions on commission or, often, at its own expense and investment.

Media Syndication Group Inc.
655 Ave. of the Americas #200
New York, NY 10010
212-924-9563

Places products in credit card inserts, catalogs, newspaper free-standing inserts, and other print advertising promotions.

Catalog Solutions, Inc.
521 Riverside Ave.
Westport, CT 06880
203-454-1919

Commissioned representatives placing products in many catalogs, such as Taylor Gifts, Hanover House, Harriet Carter, Hammacher Schlemmer, and Fingerhut, as well as with other direct-mail marketers such as Publishers Clearing House.

Publications

The Wholesale-by-Mail Catalog

This big book is updated annually, published by The Print Project, distributed by Harper Publishers, and is available in bookstores and libraries. It lists and describes over 500 catalog and mail-order companies that offer discount and wholesale prices to their customers.

Inside the Leading Mail-Order Houses

This may be the most detailed, exhaustive analysis of approximately 300 leading mail-order companies, compiled by industry expert Maxwell Scroge, and published by NTC Books (available at bookstores or through *Direct Marketing* magazine).

Oxbridge Communications Inc.
150 Fifth Ave.
New York, NY 10011
212-741-0231

Major directory publisher, including *Standard Periodical Directory*, *Directory of Newsletters*, *Directory of Catalogs*, and *Directory of Mailing Lists*. Their *National Directory of Catalogs* is indispensable to the person interested in placing his products in others' catalogs. Some of these directories may be available at your public library.

Direct Marketing Marketplace
National Register Publishing
Reed Reference Publishing Co.
121 Chanlon Rd.
New Providence, NJ 07974
800-323-6772

Lists direct-marketing firms, suppliers, and consultants involved with mail-order, TV and radio advertising, direct mail, etc.

Mail-Order Business Directory
B. Klein Publications
Box 8503
Coral Springs, FL 33075
305-752-1708

Details over 10,000 most active U.S. catalog companies, indexed by category.

Catalog Merchandiser Almanac
Box 532
Somers, NY 10589
800-859-0705

Comprehensive profiles of 430 leading mail-order houses and catalog companies. In my opinion, the best of the directories in providing the most detail about each company included.

How Can I Get on and Make Money from the Information Superhighway?

Ken McCarthy
(see chapter 8)

Ken publishes a special newsletter for on-line marketers, offers seminars and consulting services, and is available for speaking engagements on this subject. At the time this book was going to press, Ken was planning to relocate, so inquiries may be sent to Ken c/o Dan Kennedy, 5818 N. 7th St., #103, Phoenix, AZ 85014, and they will be forwarded.

Michael Enlow, P.I.
Marketing Technologies & Innovations
P.O. Drawer 429
Magnolia, MS 39652

Mr. Enlow is a famous legal investigator who has turned his investigative skills to the world of direct marketing, specifically the emerging technologies of computer networks, on-line services, BBS's, and the Internet. He has developed various products and publications having to do with electronic direct marketing. Call 800-277-6037.

Strangelove Enterprises
60 Springfield Rd.
Ottawa, Ontario K1M 1C7
Canada
613-747-6106
E-mail: mstrange@fonorola.net

Books, newsletter, and consulting regarding marketing via the Internet.

Dan Poynter
800-PARAPUB

Dan is a leading authority in the field of self-publishing and book marketing in general, as well as electronic book publishing and marketing via the information superhighway.

Rodney Buchser
FMS Direct
861 Seward St.
Hollywood, CA 90038
213-465-2363
fax: 213-465-3165

Rodney is an infomercial pioneer and producer who has produced over 200 half-hour infomercials and more than 1,000 direct-response commercials that have generated over $1 billion in sales.

Robert Mastin
Aegis Publishing Group
796-K Aquidneck Ave.
Newport, RI 02842
401-849-4200

Robert is the author of *900 KNOW-HOW*, the best, most honest, most complete how-to manual on the 900-number business.

How Can I Learn More About the Infomercial Business?

Publications

Response TV Magazine
201 E. Sandpointe Ave. #600
Santa Ana, CA 92707
714-513-8400

The trade magazine of the direct-response TV industry.

11 Sure-Fire Ways to Fail with Infomercials

This booklet has been featured in *Target* magazine, distributed by NIMA, etc., and is available free of charge from Dan Kennedy, 5818 N. 7th St., #103, Phoenix AZ 85014, on request.

Jordan-Whitney, Inc.
17300–17th St. #J111-K
Tustin, CA 92680
714-832-0737

Jordan-Whitney publishes weekly and monthly tracking reports on all infomercials and direct-response commercials, and maintains video archives of all shows and spots by product category. This is the authoritative source relied on by infomercial industry professionals.

How Can I Get My Products Sold on the Home Shopping Networks?

You can approach these companies directly, over the transom, but it is usually better to be represented by a broker with established relationships in this industry, as these companies are besieged with submissions. The requirements are rather stringent, by the way. For product evaluation, direct assistance, or referral to appropriate brokers, you can contact my office (address on page 215). It's best to do so by mail or fax (602-269-3113), not by phone.

How Can I Get Celebrities as Spokespersons or to Endorse My Products?

Celebrities can be obtained for broadcast, print advertising, and even direct mail at surprisingly affordable costs. Many celebrities are available for different kinds of projects from $5,000 to $25,000, usually plus royalties. The Academy of Motion Picture Arts Directories list most actors and actresses and their agents and managers. Most celebrity brokers can also provide contact with active and retired professional athletes, famous authors and speakers, and other non-Hollywood celebrities. I help many clients secure celebrities, and I utilize brokers, agents, and directories, plus an informal network of celebrity photographers, celebrities I've worked with, and other entertainment industry contacts for my celebrity searches for each project. If you need this kind of assistance, you are welcome to contact my office (address on page 215), and/or:

Jack King, Celebrity Broker
400 S. Beverly Dr. #214
Beverly Hills, CA 90212
310-652-5700

Marty Ingels
7080 Hollywood Blvd., 11th Floor
Hollywood, CA 90028
213-464-0800

Rick Bradley
The William Morris Agency
151 El Camino Dr.
Beverly Hills, CA 90212
310-859-4501

Leanna Levy
Cassell-Levy Inc.
843 N. Sycamore Ave.
Los Angeles, CA 90038
213-461-3971

Publications

Academy of Motion Picture Arts and Sciences Directories
Academy Players Directories
8949 Wilshire Blvd.
Beverly Hills, CA 90211
213-278-8990

How Can I Create Positive Publicity for My Business?

Publications

Working Press of the Nation
Reed Reference Publishing
121 Chanlon Rd.
New Providence, NJ 07974
908-464-6800

Lists names, addresses, phones, executives, editors, producers, hosts, etc., for 6,000+ daily and weekly newspapers, 10,000 radio and TV stations, 2,000 feature writers and syndicated columnists, etc.

Hudsons Washington News Media Contacts Directory
B. Klein Publications
Box 8503
Coral Springs, FL 33075
305-752-1708

4,500+ correspondents for wire services, news bureaus, syndicates, newspapers, etc., based in Washington, DC.

Hudsons Newsletter Directory

2,500+ U.S. and foreign newsletter publishers, by subject category, with publisher's name, address, phone, editors, size of circulation, and frequency of publication.

The Zen of Hype

Audiocassette course, manual, contact lists, etc., in a complete publicity kit prepared by Raleigh Pinskey (see chapter 10). Raleigh has developed publicity for a diverse collection of products and businesses, including the Callanetics fitness program, the $5,000 Marilyn Monroe doll, the $10,000 Elvis doll, the Bronx Zoo in New York, several daytime-TV actors and actresses, and comedian Robert Klein.

   For more information or to order *The Zen of Hype* kit, contact Empire Communications Corp., 800-223-7180. To contact Ms. Pinskey directly, write to The Raleigh Group, Ltd., 1009½–16th St., Santa Monica, CA 90403.

Services

Radio & TV Interview Report
Bradley Communications Corp.
135 E. Plumstead Ave. #125
Lansdowne, PA 19050
800-989-1400

This publication is used by radio and TV talk show producers and hosts to find guests, and you can advertise yourself in this report. Reach over 3,500 hosts and producers with an ad in this respected, effective publication. Several of my personal clients regularly advertise here with excellent results.

How Can I Get My Ads Placed at the Best Rates Possible?

You can contact just about any media directly, obtain a detailed media kit, and, if you wish, place advertising directly with that media; in some cases, this may be best. However, in many instances, you can save money and get knowledgeable assistance by dealing with media placement agencies and services.

Advertising Placement

Novus Marketing Inc.
601 Lakeshore Pkwy. #900
Minneapolis, MN 55305
612-476-7700
Attention: Tim Finley

Places direct-response display ads in major magazines, *USA Today*, and other publications at discounts from rate card of as much as 70 percent.

Page Four Media
Box 370578
West Hartford, CT 06137
203-236-6700

Arranges deeply discounted full-page advertisements in regional editions of magazines like *Time*, *Newsweek*, and *Sports Illustrated*. This allows use of major national media to target specific geographic areas. Also an affordable way to test one of these magazines before pursuing a full, national buy. A full-page ad in

Time, targeted to a particular major city, can cost less than a full-page ad in that same city's daily newspaper.

Publisher Inquiry Services
951 Broken Sound Pkwy.
Boca Raton, FL 33431
407-998-7926

Runs "Best Catalogs in the World" and other advertising programs for catalogers. You can advertise your catalog and pay for the advertising by the lead generated (per inquiry).

Associated Mail Marketers, Inc.
63 Domino Dr.
Concord, MA 01742
508-369-2316

Publishes a co-op catalog of catalogs (*Mail-Order America*) in which your catalog can be advertised, and provides catalog preparation and consulting services to catalog marketers.

Venture Communications
60 Madison Ave.
New York, NY 10010
212-684-4800
Attention: Richard Baumer

Publisher of over 250 different decks, with total circulation of over 25 million. Both consumer and business-to-business decks. Venture serves over 4,000 advertisers and is one of the largest coordinators of card deck advertising in the country.

National Mail-Order Classified
Box 5
Sarasota, CA 34230
813-366-3003

Placement of classifieds and small displays by magazine grouping. For example, one placement through NMOC can put an ad in all the women's magazines, or all the tabloids, etc., at a discount rate.

National Response Corp.
13619 Inwood Rd. #300
Dallas, TX 75244

NRC is the largest national placement agency for classified and small display advertisers, and features substantial discounts and convenience in placing ads in weekly community newspapers, shoppers, specialty magazines, even computer bulletin boards. The CEO of NRC, Phil Kratzer, is also a direct-marketing expert in his own right, and is the author, coauthor, or editor of over fifty different home-study products about different aspects of direct marketing, published by NRC. The company's frequently published "Insider Report" presents innovative advertising and marketing strategies as well as detailed descriptions of NRC's services and products.

How Can I Put Together Super-Powerful Direct-Mail Campaigns for My Business?

Better than half of all the business successes I've used as examples in this book are significantly dependent, some almost entirely dependent, on direct mail. I believe that the greatest of all favors an entrepreneur can do for himself is to learn how to effectively use direct mail to promote ideas, products, services, and businesses.

The success of a direct-mail campaign is roughly 60 percent dependent on the list, and the offer-to-list's known interests match; 30 percent dependent on the copy; and 10 percent dependent on format and appearance. The sales letter is the single most important component part of any direct-mail package.

Publications

The Ultimate Sales Letter
by Dan S. Kennedy
Published by Bob Adams Publishers, Inc.
In bookstores or call 1-800-223-7180

Features a twenty-eight-step system anybody can follow, plus numerous examples, fill-in-the-blank headlines, and other tools.

Standard Rate & Data Services (SRDS)
3004 Glenview Rd.
Wilmette, IL 60091

SRDS directories provide comprehensive detail about every commercially available mailing list. This is a fantastic resource for gathering research about a particular market; for example, by using SRDS, you can compile a profile of the typical golf products buyer: age, sex, average mail-order purchase amount, which publications he subscribes to, which publications he subscribes to most, as well as the number of potential core customers in this group. Usually, one-year-old editions of SRDS are available at major city public libraries.

Suppliers

Rocket Mail
2100 Palmetto St. #A
Clearwater, FL 34625
800-826-2869

Pre-fab, ready-to-use mailing packages that simulate Express Mail, Federal Express, etc., in envelope appearance. Proven, highly effective campaigns. Complete mailing services. Catalog, samples on request.

Response Graphics
1113 S. Milwaukee Ave.
Libertyville, IL 60048
818-501-6500

Personalized typewriter-look or handwriting-look letters and envelopes prepared. Mailing services.

Bacompt Systems Inc.
8561 Zionsville Rd.
Indianapolis, IN 46268
800-533-7109

Technology and equipment for simulated handwriting for letters, envelopes, and direct-mail campaigns.

Personalized Mailing
1835 Whittier Ave. #F6
Costa Mesa, CA 92627
714-646-7008

This computerized, automatic typewriting service can take your list and generate individually typed envelopes at rapid speed, and low cost.

How Can I Get More Help Developing and Marketing Information Products?

References

Ted Nicholas
(see chapter 9)

For information about Ted's books, newsletter, seminars, and complete audio/video home-study course on marketing information products, contact Nicholas Direct, Inc., 19918 Gulf Boulevard #7D, Indian Shores, FL 34635. One of Ted's most valuable products is a huge notebook of every ad, sales letter, postcard, etc., he ever tested and used, in selling over $200 million worth of products and services, each rated from one to five stars, indicating its success.

Gary Halbert

Gary has two publications of direct, profound relevance to the task of finding or creating a highly promotable information product: (1) the December 5, 1987 issue of *The Halbert Letter*, reprinted as chapter 2 in the current edition of his book *Maximum Money in Minimum Time*; and (2) the October 23, 1992 issue of his other newsletter, *Hot Stuff*. Gary also has information available about the CD-ROM publishing business. For information, contact Gary's office at 305-534-2508.

Melvin Powers

Melvin has self-published books and made them into bestsellers, including *Dynamic Thinking*, of which he has sold more than 1 million copies, almost entirely via mail-order, although many of his titles are also distributed in major bookstore chains, as well as—depending on their subject matter—health food stores, sporting goods stores, pet stores, and toy and hobby shops. Melvin Powers is one of the few experts in the field of information products whom I have viewed as a valid mentor, and have studied as a model in bringing my own products to market. My copy of his book *How to Self-Publish Your Book and Have the Fun and Excitement of Being a Bestselling Author* is dog-eared, yellow-highlighted, underlined, and Post-it–Noted half to death. You can and should contact Melvin Powers at 12015 Sherman Rd., Hollywood, CA 91605.

Jeff Paul
(see chapter 9)

Jeff has mastered a very special approach to mail-order and to
successfully publishing/marketing information products that I believe offers the lowest-risk, safest entry to this field of any
method or strategy.

Jeff's book, *How You Can Make $4,000.00 A Day, Sitting at
Your Kitchen Table, in Your Underwear,* is available for $29.95
plus $3.50 shipping/handling from 1-800-721-8003, ext. 904, or
by sending a check to JPDK, Inc., 121 N. Washington St., Dept.
904, Naperville, IL 60540. The book is sold on a satisfaction-
guaranteed basis.

How Can I Produce My Audio- and Videocassette Products?

LifeTech Broadcasting Corp.
5818 N. 7th St. #103
Phoenix, AZ 85014
602-997-7707

The author's video/infomercial production company can offer
turnkey services for creative development and production of
everything from simple video brochures to complex, broadcast-
quality TV infomercials.

Cassette Productions Unlimited
5796 Martin Rd.
Irwindale, CA 91706
818-969-6881
Attention: Layne Scharton

CPU is a one-stop shop, providing every service related to cassette product production under one roof. CPU is the largest supplier of such services to the infomercial industry, and specializes
in spoken-word products.

Miller Audio
Box 2282
Oglethorpe, GA 30742
800-426-8399

Blank tapes and supplies, duplicating equipment, and packaging
and duplicating services. Catalog on request.

Multi-Media Publishing & Packaging
9430 Topanga Canyon Rd. #200
Chatsworth, CA 91311
818-341-7484

Packaging supplies and services for audio- and videotapes, software, CDs, etc., both "stock" (standard) and custom items.

Video Duplication Services
384 N. 6th St.
Columbus, OH 43215
800-289-4301

Low prices, even on quantities as few as 500 copies.

Karol Media
800-526-4773

Video duplication from five to forty-five minutes in length, as
few as 100 copies at very competitive prices. Labels, mailers,
even fulfillment services available.

Promotional Video Duplicators
900 Second St. NS #110
Washington, DC 20002
800-FYI-4PVD

New "disposable" limited-use videos, for direct-mail, video
brochures—as inexpensive as $1.50 each, duplicated, labeled,

boxed, and ready to mail. These new marketing tools are exciting!

How Can I Get Set Up to Accept Major Credit Cards from My Customers?

Obtaining VISA/MasterCard merchant processing for direct-marketing businesses, especially new ones, is an increasingly vexing problem. The unfortunate truth is there is no really good answer. Persistence and patience will often be required. VISA/MC and their processing banks clearly discriminate against direct marketers.

NEW HELP FOR START-UPS

With the widespread use of 800 numbers, few catalog companies can survive today without offering credit card ordering. But just try to find a credit card processor that will take small or new cataloguers as clients. It's not easy.

Jean Hill, the founder of start-up food cataloguer, Amara Kosher Meats in New York City, says she contacted 15 processors and banks before she found one willing to take her business. Finally, New Hampshire–based Litle&Co. accepted Hill's account under the Alliance Program, a new venture designed to help start-ups and small mailers with credit processing needs. [As of August 1993] the Program has 34 mailers, 15 waiting to start.

"Litle has been so nice to deal with," says Katherine Ansardi, founder of Indelible Blue, a computer software cataloguer. She has only one complaint: "It's a little pricey," she says. "Litle requires a 10% retainer of sales that is causing us cash flow problems."

Catalog participants (in Alliance) must offer a product rather than a service and must also pass a stringent credit check and site inspection.

Charter Pacific Bank, based in Agoura, California, specializes in processing credit card transactions for new or small catalogers, which make up about 3/4s of its business. The bank also has stringent security requirements.

(*Article excerpted from* Catalog Age *magazine 8193, provided here for better understanding.*)

VISA/MC Processors

Data Processors International
9241 Bedford Ave.
Omaha, NE 68134
402-571-6199

First Premier Bank
P.O. Box 5203
Sioux Falls, SD 57117

First of Omaha—Merchant Processing
800-228-2443

Publications

How to Apply and Negotiate for Your Merchant Bankcard Account
by Nathaniel Roberts
Sales & Marketing Services
801 W. El Camino Real #265
Mountain View, CA 94040
800-305-0939

How Can I Get the Best Prices and Assistance with My Printing and Publishing Needs?

For many direct marketers, preparation and printing of sales letters, brochures, catalogs, and other promotional materials, and the publishing of books and manuals are the biggest expenses to contend with. It's extremely important to get competitive quotes and to monitor all of these costs. Also, there are printing suppliers who specialize in serving direct marketers who can usually beat local vendors' prices and delivery times, and have a better understanding of your needs.

Champion Printing Co.
3250 Spring Grove Ave.
Cincinnati, OH 45225
800-543-1957

Standard business reply envelope–order form and brochure formats; fit your piece to one of their formats and save a lot of money.

Dinner & Klein
600 S. Spokane St.
Seattle, WA 98124
800-234-6637

Largest, lowest-priced printing company I know of specializing in catalogs and direct-mail materials for the direct-marketing industry. For example: How about a sixteen-page catalog for eight cents each? They have a free production guide, sample kit, and price list available on request.

Western Web Printing
4005 S. Western Ave.
Sioux Falls, SD 57117
800-843-6805

Services very similar to those of Dinner & Klein. Some unique catalog and brochure formats.

Publicity Printing
NRS
Box 70
Kimberly, WI 54136

Lowest-cost, fastest-turnaround source I know of for b/w or color photos, photo reprints, postcards, flyers, tabloids, and catalogs on newsprint stock, all available short-run (in small quantities). They're sort of a "secret" of professional publicists and ad agencies. Free catalog available on request.

Newsletter Services Inc.
1545 New York Ave. NE
Washington, DC 20002
800-345-2611

Turnkey production and mailing of newsletters and mailing list maintenance.

Graphic Illusions
17 Shad Hole Rd.
Dennisport, MA 02639
508-760-1321
Attention: Gail Gorman

Low-cost, short-run book publishing.

Folder Factory
116A High St.
Edinburg, VA 22824
800-296-4321

Custom-designed and -printed two-pocket folders for product literature or other materials. Also special mailing envelopes and packages. Free catalog and samples on request.

Advertisers Press
6620 Lakeside Rd.
West Palm Beach, FL 33411
800-354-0022

Full-color printing, catalog sheets, brochures, and folders.

How Can I Handle Fulfillment
of the Orders I Receive?

Many companies, especially start-ups, choose to handle their in-bound order-taking and their fulfillment internally, for maximum control, maximum contact with customers, lowest costs, and loss control. My own preference is to handle as much of this hands-on, in-house, as possible. There are, however, a great many service companies that offer in-bound call services and fulfillment services.

Order Processing and Fulfillment
Service Companies

Communication Service Centers
777 S. State Rd. 7
Margate, FL 33068
800-537-8000

In-bound call management and order-taking, fulfillment, and customer service. In their Shop By Phone Division, they offer small mail-order companies a complete package of services: in-bound call and order-taking, credit card acceptance and processing (their merchant account), inventory, fulfillment, accounting, and more.

Response Call Inc.
1785 Cortland Court
Addison, IL 60101

In-bound calls, order-taking, and data-processing services.

How Can I Most Efficiently Sell by Phone to My Inquiries and Customers?

Outbound Telemarketing Service

InfoCision Management
325 Springside Dr.
Akron, OH 44333
216-668-1400
Attention: Steve Pittendrigh, V.P.

InfoCision is one of the largest and, in my opinion, highest-quality, high-volume outbound telemarketing service companies in America.

How Can I Best Build My Knowledge, Make Contacts, and Discover Opportunities Through Association?

Joining appropriate trade and professional associations, and participating in their conventions and conferences, can shorten your learning curve, help you make valuable contacts, and help you find the best vendors for your needs.

Associations

International Association of Publishers, Mail-Order Dealers and Entrepreneurs
12 Westerville Square #335D
Westerville, OH 43081
800-783-1503

Association for small, independent publishers, manufacturers, importers, and distributors utilizing classified advertising and mail-order marketing.

National Writers Club
1450 S. Havana, Suite 620
Aurora, CO 80012
303-751-7844

COSMEP
P.O. Box 420703
San Francisco, CA 94142
415-922-9490
fax: 415-922-5566

National Speakers Association
1500 S. Priest Dr.
Tempe, AZ 85281
602-968-2552
fax: 602-968-0911

National Infomercial Marketing Association
1201 New York Ave. NW #1000
Washington, DC 20005
800-962-9796

Direct Marketing Association
11 W. 42nd St.
New York, NY 10036
212-972-2410

DMA membership is quite expensive, but it is the largest association of its kind, offering a wide range of member services, a huge selection of seminars and conferences, and major annual conventions and exhibitions.

C.E.O. Clubs
180 Varick St., Penthouse
New York, NY 10014
212-633-0060

Clubs with monthly meetings, newsletters, and networking for
CEOs of companies with at least several million dollars in annual sales. Clubs currently operating in a dozen U.S. cities.

Publications

National Trade & Professional Associations Directory
Columbia Books Inc.
1212 New York Ave. NW #330
Washington, DC 20005

Profiles approximately 7,000 associations and their annual meetings and trade shows.

Directory of Conventions
Bill Communications, Inc.
355 Park Ave. South
New York, NY 10010
212-592-6438

Directory of 14,000 state, regional, and national conventions and
conferences.

What Publications Should I Read Every
Month to Stay Informed About
Direct Marketing?

Hoke Communications, Inc.
224 Seventh St.
Garden City, NY 11530
800-229-6700

Publishes *Direct Marketing* magazine and the *Direct Marketing Info-Bank Catalog*, the largest selection of audio- and videocassette interviews, profiles, and case histories of successful direct marketers ("How 1-800-FLOWERS Generates Big Sales for Flower Shops," "Joe Sugarman's Blu-Blockers Infomercial Has Sold Millions of Sunglasses").

No BS Marketing Letter/Kennedy Inner Circle

Members of the author's inner circle receive a monthly in-depth newsletter, free consulting call-in days, seminar discounts, and many other benefits. For a special discount offer for readers of this book, or to subscribe, call 800-223-7180.

Direct Marketing News
Box 3045
Langhorne, PA 19047
212-741-2095

The weekly trade publication of the direct marketing industry.

InfoText Publishing
34700 Coast Highway #309
Capistrano Beach, CA 92624

Publishes *INFOTEXT*, the trade magazine of the 800 and 900 number information provider (IP) businesses.

Catalog Age
911 Hope St.
Stamford, CT 06907
800-795-5445

Monthly trade magazine for professionals in the catalog business. Also a library of books relevant to the catalog business.

The Halbert Letter
820 Ocean Drive #308
Miami Beach, Florida 33139
305-534-2508

Monthly how-to and opinion newsletter on direct-response advertising, direct-mail, and direct-marketing written by Gary Halbert (see chapter 7).

Additional General Publications

It is my opinion that you are not doing your job as an entrepreneur if you fail to read Success magazine, Inc. magazine, Entrepreneur magazine, Business Week, the Wall Street Journal, and USA Today (at least frequently, if not daily).

Other Sources of Information

ABI Network
5711 S. 86th Circle
Omaha, NE 68127
800-808-INFO

ABI provides business directory assistance nationwide, when the regular telephone company operators can't help you. For example, let's say you need the names of gift shops or trophy stores or Ford dealers in a particular city . . . or you know the company name and state, but not the city. ABI can provide this type of information, by phone or fax for fees. You can also obtain corporate profiles and credit reports through ABI.

Directories in Print
Gale Research
835 Penobscot Bldg.
Detroit, MI 48226
800-877-GALE

A master guide to all business, industrial, professional, association, and service directories. Gale also publishes *The Encyclopedia of Associations*, *Wards Business Directory*, and a 65,000-
entry database of publications. For a free sample diskette, call
800-877-GALE.

Guide to American Directories
B. Klein Publications
Box 8503
Coral Springs, FL 33075
305-752-1708

200 classifications, 8,000 different directories profiled and cross-
indexed.

The Popcorn Report

Faith Popcorn has been mentioned several times in this book.
Her book *The Popcorn Report* is must reading for every entrepreneur. Her success at predicting societal trends and relating
them to product and business development in a practical way is
unmatched.

Other books in this category include John Naisbitt's *Mega-
trends 2000*, Michael Weiss's *The Clustering of America*, and Al-
vin Toffler's *Powershift*. *American Demographics* magazine also
forecasts trends for business purposes.

Doctoral Dissertations

You may find lots of information about any given subject buried
in doctoral dissertations from universities nationwide. A free catalog of available dissertations is offered by University Microfilms
International, 800-521-0600.

Small Business Administration and Free Government Assis-
tance for Entrepreneurs

By starting with the SBA's answer line, 800-827-5722, or SBA ONLINE, 800-697-4636, you can find all the many available government documents, publications, resources, and services, locations of government bookstores, SCORE (Service Corps of Retired Executives) free consulting services, and much more.

Another excellent resource for finding hundreds of sources of information, including government agencies' 800 numbers, is Matthew Lesko's book *Info-Power*. You can get information about all of Matthew's publications from Information USA, Inc., Box E, Kensington, MD 20895.

Further Resources

Chapter 2

Murray Raphel
Raphel Marketing
12 S. Virginia Ave.
Atlantic City, NJ 08401
609-348-6646
fax: 609-347-2455

Any and every business owner can benefit from reading Murray's books and attending one of his seminars.

Bob Stupak
Vegas World Hotel
2000 Las Vegas Blvd. South
Las Vegas, NV 89104
702-382-2000

Larry Harmon
CEO
De-Mar Plumbing
205 W. Pontiac Way
Clovis, CA 93612
209-298-7944

Chapter 3

Good Sam Club
c/o TL Enterprises Inc.
3601 Calle Tecate
Camarillo, CA 93012

Tom Doyle
Gripping Solutions, Inc.
4141 Pinnacle, Suite 210
El Paso, TX 79902

Joseph Cossman
Cossman International, Inc.
Box 4480
Palm Springs, CA 92263

Joe Cossman's "exploits"—and they honestly can be called nothing less—have been a constant source of inspiration to me since I first read his book *How I Made $1,000,000 in Mail-Order and You Can, Too* over twenty years ago. More recently, it was a privilege to get to know him personally, in connection with an infomercial project. And, even though in his old age I found him to be irascible and difficult to deal with, I have to tell you that, in my experience, no one has as much practical experience in turning raw ideas, orphaned and odd products, and information into fortunes.

Wilson Call
Wilson Call Inc.
2200 F St.
Bakersfield, CA 93301
805-322-4686

This inventor's determination paid off! Since its invention, over 250,000 Fireplugs have been sold through hardware, drug, and discount stores; catalogs like Carol Write and Herringtons; and Wilson's own direct advertising and publicity. (You can order a

Fireplug or a copy of his book, *The Anatomy of an Invention*,
directly from Wilson Call Inc. for $7.95 plus $1.50 shipping and
handling.)

Jim Winner
President
Winner International Corporation
Manufacturers of THE CLUB
32 West State St.
Sharon, PA 16146

Chapter 4

Woody Young
Joy Publishing
10893 San Paco Circle
Fountain Valley, CA 92708
714-962-8611

Chapter 5

Carl Galetti
Lord and Collins
One Paddock Dr.
Lawrenceville, NJ 08648
609-896-0245

Note: Carl will send you a free catalog of his hard-to-find, classic
books on advertising and marketing, on request.

Earl Nightingale
Nightingale-Conant Inc.
7300 N. Lehigh Ave.
Chicago, IL 60648
800-323-5552

The late Earl Nightingale was one of the early pioneers in "success education." His record "The Strangest Secret" literally launched an industry. Earl's classic cassettes, including "The Strangest Secret" and "Lead the Field," are still available from the company he cofounded, which has become the leading publisher of business and self-improvement–related spoken-word products.

Rory Fatt
Simple Salmon, Inc.
311-810 W. Broadway
Vancouver, B.C. V5Z 4C9
Canada

Micheline Massé
President
StockSearch International, Inc.
10855 N. Glen Abbey Dr.
Tucson, AZ 85737
602-544-2590

Val-Pak Direct Marketing Systems, Inc.
8605 Largo Lakes Drive
Largo, FL 34643
813-393-1170

James A. Smith
President
Journal Graphics, Inc.
Denver, Colorado

Chapter 6

Mark Colosi
The Wealth Factory
1057 E. Henrietta Rd.
Rochester, NY 14623
716-273-8000

Gary Haiser
President
Personal Wealth Systems, Inc.
8535 Baymeadows Rd., Suite 25-K1
Jacksonville, FL 32256
904-731-5785, ext. K1

Laurence J. Pino
Chairman
The Open University
24 S. Orange Ave., Dept. 17D
Orlando, FL 32801
407-649-8488

Leonard C. Shykind
President
U.S. Gold Chain Manufacturing, Inc.
11460 N. Cave Creek Rd., Dept. #73
Phoenix, AZ 85020
602-971-1243, ext. #73

Chapter 7

Steve Pittendrigh
Vice President, Direct Response Marketing
InfoCision Management
325 Springside Dr. #MM1
Akron, OH 44333
216-668-1400, ext. #MM1

Carol Curtis & Peter Deutsch
Creative Bird Accessories Catalog
Box 2157
Darien, CT 06820

Gary Halbert
820 Ocean Dr. #308
Miami Beach, FL 33139
305-534-2508

Chapter 8

Napoleon Hill

You probably are already very familiar with Napoleon Hill. For the uninitiated: As a young man, Napoleon Hill was sent on a twenty-year mission by Andrew Carnegie, America's first billionaire, to personally interview and spend time with hundreds of the greatest achievers of their time in search of the unanimously shared secrets of success. The report of his findings, *Think and Grow Rich!*, first published in 1937, has been a perennial bestselling book entirely through word-of-mouth recommendation. You *must* read *Think and Grow Rich!*, which is available in bookstores.

Tony Robbins

If you've watched late-night television anytime in the past five years, you have undoubtedly seen Tony with Fran Tarkenton, Martin Sheen, and many celebrities discussing the benefits of his Personal Power Program. Well over $50 million worth of Personal Power Programs have been sold through these TV infomercials alone. You can get information on Personal Power from the Guthy-Renker Corporation. Tony's books *Unlimited Power* and *Awaken the Giant Within* are available in bookstores.

Greg Renker
CEO
Guthy-Renker Corporation
41-550 Eclectic, Suite 200
Palm Desert, CA 92260
619-773-9022

Mark Kress
President
Joan Rivers Products
113A Post Road East
Westport, CT 06880

Peter Herrold
President
Perfect Swing Trainer, Inc.
5768 S. Semoran Blvd.
Orlando, FL 32822
407-249-7722

Chapter 9

Ted Nicholas

See How Can I Get Help Developing and Marketing Information
Products?

Ted Thomas
New Growth Financial
Box 490
Danville, CA 94526

John Mortz
818-568-4700

This number connects you to John's twenty-four-hour, free recorded message about his Moonlighting Advisor products for
people interested in making money at home with their
computers.

Bob Burg
Burg Communications Inc.
Box 7002
Jupiter, FL 33468

Chapter 10

Tim and Wendy Eidson
Mo Hotta–Mo Betta
Box 4136
San Luis Obispo, CA 93430
800-462-3220

Sheryl Leach & "Barney"
The Lyons Group
300 E. Bethany Rd.
Allen, Texas 75002

Al Parinello
50 Greenwoods
Old Tappan, NJ 07675

Al's excellent book, *On the Air: How to Get on Radio and TV Talk Shows and What to Do When You Get There*, is available in bookstores or by calling 201-784-0059.

Joe and Judy Sabah
P.O. Box 101330
Denver, CO 80250
303-722-7200

Lee Milteer
Lee Milteer Associates
P.O. Box 5653
Virginia Beach, VA 23455
804-460-1818

Mark Skousen
Forecasts and Strategies
7811 Montrose Rd.
Potomac, MD 20854

Laura Corn
c/o Park Ave. Publishers
Box 20010
Oklahoma City, OK 73156

Chapter 11

T. Harv Eker
The Street Smart Business School
1155 Camino Del Mar, #520
Del Mar, CA 92014

Communicating with the Author

Dan Kennedy welcomes your communication. He is available, schedule permitting, for speaking and seminar engagements, consulting, copywriting assignments, and video and infomercial production projects. To contact Dan Kennedy concerning any of these or similar matters, it is best to write or, if speed is important, to fax. You may write to Dan Kennedy at 5818 N. 7th St., #103, Phoenix, AZ 85014, or fax to 602-269-3113 twenty-four hours a day, seven days a week. His office phone number is 602-997-7707.

On page 248 there is a coupon for *free* copies of two of Dan Kennedy's books, one of which includes a copy of his book/cassette catalog. If you wish to purchase any of his products described in this chapter before receiving the information via this coupon, you can call his order service at 800-223-7180, 10:00 A.M.–4:00 P.M. eastern standard time, on weekdays.

Coupons for Free Resources

There is no need to damage or destroy your book. Feel free to photocopy these pages and use the photocopies as your coupons.

FREE

Product Marketing
Evaluation
($500 Consultation Value)

This certificate entitles you to send a
brief description of your product, photos, literature, etc., with your specific
questions about marketing your product
—Dan Kennedy will personally review
and evaluate your information—and you
will receive a customized report including marketing recommendations.

Name _____

Address _____

City, State, Zip _____

Phone _____

FAX _____

Allow 2 to 4 Weeks—By Mail Only—
No Confidentiality Guaranteed

Send to: Dan Kennedy
5818 N. 7th St., #130
Phoenix, AZ 85014

FREE

This certificate entitles you to *free* copies of these books, on request:

1. *Yes, You Can Get Rich—Fast* by Dan Kennedy

This book features in-depth descriptions of all of Dan's services, seminars, home-study courses, audio- and videocassettes, books, and newsletters, and includes features on: "The Money System" (How to Get the Money You Need for Any Business Venture), Exceptional Results Selling, Magnetic Marketing, and Million-Dollar Thinking.

2. *How to Solve All Your Advertising, Marketing and Sales Problems—Fast and Forever.*

This book describes Dan's favorite strategies for lead generation advertising and multistep follow-up marketing.

Name _____

Address _____

City, State, Zip _____

Phone _____

FAX _____

To Obtain Both of These Books Free,
Fax This Form to: 602-269-3113
Or Mail to: Dan Kennedy,
5818 N. 7th St., #103, Phoenix, AZ 85014

Acknowledgments and Important Notices

This book would not exist without the assistance of my wife, Carla, my research assistant, Lucinda Burke, and the generous sharing of information by many of my clients and colleagues.

My attention was drawn to certain people and companies discussed in this book by articles in the following publications: *Catalog Age*, *Direct*, *Entrepreneur* magazine, *Fortune*, *The Hollywood Reporter*, *Inc.* magazine, *National Enquirer*, *Publishers Weekly*, *Success* magazine, and *Your Company*. Books that have been of special assistance or influence include Michael Gershman's *Getting It Right the Second Time Around* and Gerardo Joffe's *How You Too Can Make a Million Dollars in Mail-Order*. Special contributions from Gary Halbert, Ken McCarthy, and Rory Fatt are appreciated.

A long list of trademarks, brand names, and corporate identities have been mentioned in this book, and I want to acknowledge and appropriately caution readers that these are properties of their owners, are legally protected, and may not be used without appropriate permissions. The following trademarks have been referenced in this book:

AccessLinks
AlphaGraphics
Amazing Discoveries
America OnLine
American Express

Amoco
Amway
Animal Crackers
AT&T
Barney
Bass Pros Shops
Betty Crocker
Big Green Clean Machine, The
Blu-Blockers
Burger King
Caddylak Systems
Canned Alaskan Earthquake
Celex/Celex Group, Inc.
CLUB, THE
CompuServe
Creating Excellence
Culligan
Day-Timers
Desktop Lawyer, The
Diners Club
Dixie Cups
Domino's Pizza
The Door Club
Dunkin' Donuts
Duracell
Eagle Day Planner
Easy Glider
Endurance
Fitnessland
Fit One
Flying Lure
Franklin Planners
FTD
Gold By The Inch
Great Quotations
Gripping Solutions
Grizzly's Gifts
Hammacher Schlemmer

Prodigy
Pro-Swing System
Recipe Detective
Ronald McDonald
Satan's Revenge
Schweppes (Schweppervescence)
Seven-Up (7UP)
Sharper Image, The
Slim-Fast ("Give Us a Week and We'll Take Off the Weight")
Smith & Hawken
Spiegel
StairClimber
Subway
Successories
Sybervision
Texaco
ThighMaster
Timex
Tupperware
UNCOLA
Val-Pak
VISA
Volkswagen
White Castle
Win, Lose Or Draw

Every effort has been made to verify the accuracy of all the information contained in this book, but delays between writing and publication, and between publication and your reading of the book, guarantee there will be inaccuracies.

Index